STALIN MUST HAVE PEACE

Books by Edgar Snow

FAR EASTERN FRONT

LIVING CHINA

RED STAR OVER CHINA

THE BATTLE FOR ASIA

PEOPLE ON OUR SIDE

THE PATTERN OF SOVIET POWER

STALIN MUST HAVE PEACE

BY
EDGAR SNOW

With an Introduction by
MARTIN SOMMERS
FOREIGN EDITOR
THE SATURDAY EVENING POST

RANDOM HOUSE · NEW YORK

First Printing

ACKNOWLEDGMENT

The Introduction and Chapters I, II and III
of this book originally appeared as articles
in *The Saturday Evening Post*. Edgar Snow
and Martin Sommers express their apprecia-
tion to the editors and publishers of that
journal for permission to bring their work
together in this volume.

CONTENTS

INTRODUCTION

by

MARTIN SOMMERS

WINSTON CHURCHILL is the world's best talker and the world's most ambitious military strategist. He demonstrated his claim to both these distinctions in the White House at Washington on a June night in 1942. The salesmanship impregnated in Churchill's magic words that night probably changed the history of the world for keeps, though the change effected is not one the former Tory Prime Minister of Great Britain finds at all to his taste, judging by his recent public utterances.

The story of what happened that June night in the White House actually began two months earlier in London. In April of 1942, Harry Hopkins, acting as the eyes, ears and mouthpiece of President Franklin Delano Roosevelt, headed a military mission of first importance on a flight to London. It included Gen. George C. Marshall and some of his staff. Hopkins, Marshall & Co. took a plan with them. It was a bold one, a cross-Channel invasion of the continent of Europe in early July of 1943, not 1944. The immediate target would be Normandy, with landings on both sides of the Vire River at the base

9

of the Cherbourg Peninsula. Most of the Allied
shipping, air power, fire power and manpower available by midsummer of 1943 would be massed for
the all-out operation, with the fighting on the Pacific
war to progress at quarter to half speed until the
Germans were totally defeated. General Marshall
believed in the plan as the logical implement to
achieve his simple and often-repeated objective, "to
win the war as quickly and as economically as possible." But it had to be sold to the British High
Command, the British Cabinet, and, of course,
Churchill.

General Marshall went right to work at first
contact with the British with one of those clear,
brilliant expositions for which he is celebrated.
There was considerable opposition, especially during
a series of heated debates at 10 Downing Street,
one attended by King George VI. But finally the
British agreed to the cross-Channel operation as
planned for 1943. Hopkins, Marshall & Co. were
delighted, and flew home more optimistic than they
had been seen since before Pearl Harbor. They were
set to pour it on for '43, and platoons of planners
of detail went to work.

But after they left England, something happened
—something very strange, as it turned out. On June

3, 1942, Lord Louis Mountbatten arrived in Washington to be the guest of the President at the White House. Lord Louis, an affable storyteller, is the kind of convivial aristocrat for whom President Roosevelt always had a soft spot. He invariably called him "Dicky," as members of the royal family did. Mountbatten made good use of the hospitality he enjoyed. One day not long after his arrival he talked to the President for five hours at a single stretch, and all of that time he talked against the cross-Channel operation planned for 1943. He had misgivings, forebodings, doubts and finally firm arguments.

The news of what he was doing reached informed circles of our armed services. It didn't make them happy, but there was nothing for them to do except go ahead according to plan—and agreement.

Mountbatten had the run of the White House for a fortnight—and then came Churchill. The Prime Minister arrived on June eighteenth and fell comfortably into the place that Mountbatten had gone before to prepare for him. He, too, was now definitely against the cross-Channel operation in 1943.

Churchill went to work at unselling the President —the man who was, after all, the sole proprietor of the necessary air, fire and manpower—on the wisdom of a '43 assault on *Festung Europa*. The inspired British leader was enthusiastic about an alternative grand strategy, one of his own. He argued eloquently that the first blow should not be delayed a full year; in any case, that the Allies, particularly the British, couldn't afford to continue to feed and keep great masses of troops inactive for a full year, with the general public clamoring for action, and in need of an offensive to bolster morale. The immediate solution was to strike as soon as possible in 1942 in the Mediterranean area, perhaps in North Africa. Then, after the Germans were pinched out of North Africa, the next successive steps should be the mop-up of the Mediterranean islands, the occupation of Southern Italy, and the invasion of the Continent through the Balkans. It was during these sessions that the Prime Minister coined a fine new phrase, "the soft underbelly of Europe"—one which later led our soldiers, pinned down in the blood, ice and mud of the Italian mountains, to remark that what Mr. Churchill didn't know about the tensile strength of bellies was a great plenty.

Churchill's strategy was an old and familiar one, that control of Europe should be won by invasion along the historic Belgrade-Warsaw axis of attack.

He put his emphasis on the strategical military reasons why this route to the destruction of the Wehrmacht and the occupation of Germany should be taken. But his two main reasons for advocating such a course were political. Both had to do with the interests of the British Empire—interests which the British Prime Minister only naturally considered paramount at all times.

In that summer of 1942 the British Government was greatly worried about its tetchy relations with Australia, Egypt, India and South Africa. The government, too, was gravely concerned about how much more the little people of the home islands, despite the matchless durability they had displayed, could take. Britannia was sick, abroad, in the Empire, and at home. The strategy the Prime Minister had conceived would be a partial cure for both maladies. If the British won a firm position on both sides of the Mediterranean, securing the lifeline of the Empire to a degree it never had boasted even in peacetime, obviously Australia and South Africa would be mightily heartened and India and Egypt more securely bound to the Empire. If the war could be kept as far as possible away from the home islands, giving the little people there a chance to draw a few tranquil breaths, their waning powers of resistance would revive, they would get their second wind and return to the struggle with vim and will. Moreover, if these things were accomplished, Canada, where the civilian population had grown impatient with the progress of the war—as civilian populations will—would be reassured, and respond to a note of triumph with a confident redoubling of effort. From Churchill's point of view, his strategy was precisely what the doctor ordered, and he was able in his own mind to make strictly military considerations conform to the pattern his imaginative brain had created.

The Prime Minister had had only a few after-dinner sessions with President Roosevelt when, a few minutes after ten o'clock that fateful June night, the White House secretariat began calling all hands. They were the top hands—General Marshall and Admiral Ernie King and Gen. H. H. Arnold and their immediate assistants—the men charged with the conduct of the American offensive on the land, at sea and in the air. General Marshall had to drive over from Fort Myer, in near-by Virginia, where he lived in a modest home on officers' row, with the subordinates on whom he leaned heaviest in surrounding houses, so that he could get them together quickly for any emergency, night or day.

The summons at that late hour of the night did not surprise these members of the high command especially. Churchill's penchant for beginning vital conferences well after dinner and prolonging them to a decision during the early-morning hours was no longer a novelty. In fact, some time later it became fashionable at Gen. Dwight D. Eisenhower's headquarters in London and North Africa to refer to some new and dazzling operation, boldly and suddenly sprung on the military men charged with its execution, as "one of the Prime's three-o'clock-in-the-morning decisions."

When the Americans came into the presence of the President and the Prime Minister, they found the full complement of the Anglo-American supreme board of strategy in attendance, bulwarked by their most expert advisers on the technological facets of mass destruction. At the far end of the large assembly room, the end where the teacher usually sits in a class room, was a giant easel with an elaborate detailed map of the world on it. When quiet had settled on the room and its occupants, the President from his chair near the easel invited Mr. Churchill to present a strategic review. The Prime Minister, complete with cigar, took position before the map. He embarked on a long and sometimes impassioned argument. Some of those who were present say they consider that evening's address the greatest speech Winston Churchill ever made.

The Prime's argument was that 1943 might be too early to attempt an all-out cross-Channel operation. German might was unimpaired. His implication was that such a move could prove to be another Dunkirk on a colossal scale, the kind of disaster which would prolong the war indefinitely. He made his point that, anyway, an offensive was required before 1943. Then he mobilized all the great oratorical and histrionic talent he possesses to drive home his idea for a great sweep into North Africa and up from the Mediterranean through Belgrade and to Warsaw. And as his words flowed and his pointer moved across the map in broad strokes, there emerged the picture of the Balkans, Italy and most of Europe occupied and controlled by victorious Anglo-American armies, with Russia shut out of the Adriatic and Mediterranean, and confined to her pre-war borders. In his final summation, Mr. Churchill used all the arguments he and Mountbatten had previously dinned into President Roosevelt, and added a few new ones.

Some of the American Navy bigwigs there present wore an I-told-you-so expression. They had always been skeptical of British earnestness in the matter of a 1943 cross-Channel invasion, even after the firm decision reached in London in April, and, because of their doubts, they had been quietly fighting the allocation of all types of shipping to European waters, holding out what they could for their own war in the Pacific.

The American Army chieftains simply looked grim. They had feared the worst, on the basis of what they had heard about the Mountbatten-Churchill descent on the White House, and this was it. The Prime had cleverly avoided getting the President's well-advertised Dutch up by never ruling out a cross-Channel operation in 1943 entirely. Throughout his discourse Churchill allowed the President to believe that the operations he was describing might not militate against a cross-Channel operation in 1943 after all, if such an offensive looked practical later. But the Army planners knew only too well the immense amount of shipping, fire power, air power, manpower, and so on, an invasion of North Africa and Mediterranean diversions would require. They well knew they could not possibly launch a Mediterranean offensive late in 1942 and be ready for the cross-Channel invasion in 1943. And they knew that Churchill—with a far greater knowledge of strategy, tactics and logistics than President Roosevelt—knew it too.

When Churchill concluded, President Roosevelt called on General Marshall. The Chief of Staff unhesitatingly turned toward a tall lean colonel seated behind him, a junior officer in such company, and announced that the colonel would state the American case for the all-out cross-Channel operation in 1943, and against any prior diversions.

General Marshall made no careless choice of a spokesman. The colonel was Albert Coady Wedemeyer, now a lieutenant general commanding the 2nd Army Area. Because of the capacities he exhibited when attending the Army's Command and General Staff School at Leavenworth, Kansas, Wedemeyer had been picked to attend the German War College in Berlin. He had studied diligently there during an eventful period in the development of Germany's military might—from August of 1936 to June of 1938. One of his instructors in the Kriegsakadamie was Alfred Jodl, who afterward became one of the Reich's great strategists—and finally finished his career at the end of a hangman's rope. Wedemeyer's opportunities for absorbing the Wehrmacht's concepts of strategy and tactics were unlimited, because the American student was given the same unrestricted instruction as the 200 hand-picked German officers attending classes and working out maneuvers in the field.

Wedemeyer made the most of these opportunities. When he returned to this country he wrote a painstaking 100-page report of what he had learned, but found, somewhat to his chagrin, that his superiors in the War Department, with one exception, did not appear to be much interested. The exception was then Brigadier General Marshall. General Marshall was avidly interested in everything in the document. His interest took a practical turn when, in 1940, he suddenly summoned Wedemeyer to Washington and made him one of his key planners. As such, Wedemeyer had helped prepare the plan for the 1943 cross-Channel operation and had fought for its adoption at the conferences in London the previous April. There, at some of the more heated sessions, his statements at times had angered Churchill, but the Prime Minister's irritation at having his views opposed had left the American officer unabashed and unawed. So General Marshall could be sure that his spokesman would pull no punches at this critical command performance.

Wedemeyer proceeded with a restrained point-by-point demolition of the Prime Minister's arguments for a surge from the Mediterranean along the historic Belgrade-Warsaw axis. Where Churchill had dealt in grandiloquent generalities, Wedemeyer replied in painfully precise specifics. He offered factual and statistical evidence to support his contention that the shipping available could not give such an offensive from the Mediterranean the impetus to carry it to Warsaw. He discussed the grim character of the terrain along the road to Warsaw, the insufficiency of air-base sites to insure the required air canopies for the various steps of the offensive, the nettlesome problems of logistics.

Then Wedemeyer turned to his positives—the reasons for an all-out offensive across the Channel into France, and up through Germany into Poland, in 1943. He had been living, eating and sleeping this subject for a year. He brought to bear all he had learned at the German War College, all he had studied about the possibilities of Russian offensives at the same time, and he had in his head all the ammunition the intelligence services had been collecting for him for many months. He quoted impressive figures to show how, with the war in the Pacific slowed down, we would have enough—in shipping, in air power, in fire power and in manpower—of what it would take to do the job in 1943. Some of those present during the dramatic debate that fateful evening believe that Wedemeyer won the argument, on its merits as such.

What developed subsequently as a result of that session is too intricate and involved to relate here. Only two major results need concern us. Churchill, because of his influence on President Roosevelt, won his fight to avoid a cross-Channel operation in 1943. He lost on his determination to force an offensive via Belgrade to Warsaw—to an extent, because when the Russians heard about this plan, they raised shrill objections. But Churchill did a little better than break even. As a compromise on his pet Balkan plan he eventually won President Roosevelt's consent to the invasion of Sicily, and the long, bitter fight up the boot of Italy, as an immediate follow-up on the North African campaign.

Today, though they do not say so publicly as yet, some of our ablest military leaders believe that the North African invasion and the whole ghastly Italian campaign were unnecessary and that the dawn of VE-Day was delayed—with all that means in terms of loss of life and national treasure—by our failure to attack across the Channel in 1943. They feel reasonably certain that, with German lines strung out wide and thin against the Russians, the Anglo-

American armies could have swept through France, over all of Germany and far into Poland, Austria and Czechoslovakia. This would have left Great Britain and the United States, instead of Russia, in control of the part of Europe that counts, with Italy sealed off in surrender. In short, because of our failure to follow through on the plan to invade Europe in 1943, Russia has the drop on us in Europe today. Ironically, according to this conclusion, if the Russians had got the western offensive for which they were bellowing in the summer of 1943, they would not have been very happy about the result.

A full post-mortem discussion of the pros and cons of what the proponents of this idea contend would fill volumes. But a few of the indubitable facts they present are very impressive. For example, the records now show that in the summer of 1943 the Germans had only twenty-nine divisions available in France and the Low Countries to oppose an invasion. When we landed in Normandy in 1944 they had fifty-eight divisions available in those areas, or double the total in 1943. In addition, because we waited a year, the Germans had that extra time to strengthen the formidable structural defenses of the beaches and their so-called West Wall. Moreover, some of our military's guesses as to what the Russians could be calculated to do to the Wehrmacht during the winter of 1942-43 proved accurate. The entire German 6th Army was encircled and destroyed at Stalingrad during that winter, and the terrifying German might, which Mountbatten and Churchill envisaged as a deterrent to a cross-Channel operation in the summer of 1943, no longer existed when that summer rolled around.

Whatever the right and wrong of the historic decision in the White House that June night, the over-all result we face today is clear. We do not enjoy the position of advantage we would have enjoyed, vis-à-vis Russia, had the Anglo-American armies swept over all of Germany and into Czechoslovakia, Austria and Poland, and been there in possession when hostilities ended in Europe. Russia today has the drop on us in Europe and enjoys a vast sphere of influence in a world which has not yet forsworn the practices of power politics. Whatever we may think about it, the Soviet rulers believe their new place in the sun, a position of power undreamed of by even the most ambitious of the tsars, is their rightful heritage, bought by the blood of 7,000,000 Russians. And Russia is taking every advantage of this belief, to the fullest.

The first great advantage—one that transcends all others as the Russians see it—is the chance to insure themselves forever against encirclement. I am aware that in doing his paper work—the periodical filling-out of questionnaires submitted to him —Generalissimo Stalin has stated that Russia need not fear encirclement. It is my belief, based on conversations with Russians in positions of authority —conversations which antedated the word from the Generalissimo—that the fear of encirclement haunts the dialectic materialists who rule Russia just as relentlessly, say, as a congenital inferiority complex used to haunt the former rulers of Japan. One of the franker of the Russian officials I interviewed, pressed as to why Hitler and Stalin made their whilom alliance, suddenly burst out with the explanation that the U.S.S.R. was being encircled, that the Soviet had to have some kind of ally on the menacing periphery, that Great Britain and the United States had snubbed Moscow, and that the Nazis were a choice of necessity.

Stalin's statement, it seems to me, was intended primarily for home consumption. It came at a time when the average Russian was in deadly fear of war, and something had to be done to calm him. And, through the statement, Stalin could drive home

the idea to his toiling masses that, if he could per-
severe in the pugnacious policy he is now following
to its logical conclusions in terms of power, controls
and spheres of influence, then indeed a vastly expanded Russia would be free of encirclement. In
short, for purposes of heartening his war-weary
people, he found it expedient to pronounce the goal
already won on the political front, with merely more
hard work by the muzhiks needed to consolidate the
victory.

It is equally true that we Americans fear encirclement by Russian-dominated communism, and it is
dishonest as well as foolish to deny this. This fear
of encirclement and the attending determination not
to take any chances with such an eventuality is the
real reason we are resisting Russian expansion
beyond certain fixed limits throughout the world.

It is the reason why our soldiers stand facing
Russian soldiers on the other side of the thirty-
eighth parallel in Korea. It is the reason why there
are no Russian occupation troops in Japan. True,
we invited them to send a token force, but on such
terms that it was a foregone conclusion they would
decline the invitation. It is the reason why until recently we had our marines on duty in North China,
and a strong and influential military mission advising

and training Generalissimo Chiang Kai-shek's ground and air forces. It is the reason why Lt. Gen. Geoffrey Keyes is keeping a watchful eye on the Russians in Vienna. It is the reason why we have stiffened our position in Germany. It is the reason why we have not given up any really important air or naval bases in any part of the world, though our get-the-boys-home policy has weakened a good many of them to the point of impotence.

Because of mutual fear and distrust, and the steps both we and the Russians have taken to implement such fear and distrust with demonstrations of force and power, what can only be called a war psychosis has been engendered. Nobody who has been willing to examine the evidence in areas of the world where we meet face to face with the Russians can deny that we are at present under political and economic attack from them. At times we have done our best to retaliate, though it has been a somewhat feeble best because in such bouts we traditionally wear twelve-ounce gloves while the untutored Russians are addicted to bare-knuckle engagements.

Though recently there has been some surcease from the alarms, you still hear talk of war everywhere you go in this country. From the lecture platform and in the newspapers you are told that

26

the hour is late, it is five minutes to twelve, war is imminent, it is upon us, any day, any hour, now.

That is dangerous and it is silly. For, putting together all the information our best intelligence services have been able to gather, you find that at this moment Russia simply cannot go to war with us, no matter what the desires of the men who rule Russia. Russia has not got what it takes—the air power, the sea power, the fire power, the industrial production, the transportation, the food, the clothing, the manpower itself. The fact is, all the evidence shows, war-ravaged Russia is far weaker today than the average American believes, simply because the Soviet rulers have taken great pains to conceal their weaknesses. And the men of the Politburo, all of them sagacious students of these matters, have just had a most impressive demonstration of what happens to great land armies when they are pitted against overwhelming air and sea power—in fact there were two demonstrations, one in each hemisphere. About the only chance of war with Russia in the next year, or two, or three, is if Generalissimo Stalin should suddenly go crazy and start his armies marching before the thirteen other members of the Politburo could get him into a strait jacket.

But just as surely, the course of Russo-American

relations is toward war at some distant date. Political and economic attacks, generating irritations and incidents over a long period until a state of animosity becomes deep and chronic, invariably lead to military attack and counterattack. It is quite probable that in fifteen years Russia will have recovered from World War II wounds, will have acquired a stockpile of atomic bombs and will be strong enough on the sea and in the air to risk war. If that war comes, it will, of course, mean the extermination of human civilization as we know it today, and it probably will come unless we do something to change the present course of our relations with Russia. In short, it isn't five minutes to twelve, it's only about half past one—but now is the time to wage peace.

And how do we Americans go about the business of waging peace? The first step is to stick on the job we undertook when we entered the war, and to make it clear to the Soviet that we are sticking. We intervened with other nations in the mission of managing the world, and it is now up to us to fulfill that responsibility. The Russians are prone to think that before long we will revert to what James Reston, the astute national correspondent of the *New York Times*, has called the "preach-and-run" policy we followed after World War I. What we should substitute for a preach-and-run policy today is a squawk-and-stick policy. If we pulled out of the competition anywhere in the world today, the Oriental-minded rulers of Russia would surely consider this as proof of our decadence and weakness. Such a conviction on their part would be certain to intensify their aggressive expansion, to our further disadvantage.

As we pursue the policy of squawk and stick, the first thing to decide is what we are going to stick to and what we are going to squawk about. In the past, we have had considerable difficulty in determining this. In the past this difficulty has stemmed from a simple fact quite apparent to most observers for some time: Our Department of State and our War Department for a long time had two different foreign policies, with each inclined to march off at oblique angles to the other.

Fundamentally, the War Department approach to problems is a soldier's approach, with the issues in black and white; the Department of State's approach under the domination of Secretary James Byrnes was a politician's approach, with everything in the grays. It is fashionable among our intellectuals to snap up a chance stupid remark of some obscure general serving out his time, blow it up out of all proportion, and represent it as typical of the mental processes of all military men. The fact is, on the record, our military men have shown a greater capacity for understanding the fine print in the treaties and making canny decisions than the majority of our diplomats. Where among the career men of the Department of State could you find men of the proved capacity of General Marshall, General Eisenhower, General MacArthur, Lt. Gen. Walter Bedell Smith, Lt. Gen. Wedemeyer or Maj. Gen. Lucius D. Clay? You think immediately of our Ambassador Robert D. Murphy, to Germany. But after that you just think, and think, and think. Nobody in our Department of State has ever been accused of anything like the diplomatic coup Lieutenant General Smith pulled off when he engineered the surrender of Italy in the negotiations at Lisbon. It is possible, of course, that because our new position in world affairs resulted from the conduct of war, and not from the conduct of diplomatic maneuver, able men in the Department of State have been obscured and submerged by the gaudier reputations of the military figures. If so, they should be unveiled.

To unify the clashing foreign policies of the State and War departments always has been a job for the White House, but the White House took no effective action until General Marshall was appointed to succeed Secretary Byrnes. It is to be hoped—and it can be expected—that Secretary Marshall will take swift action to clear up the situation, and that the foreign policy which will emerge will be a unified American policy, in plan and in operation too. Marshall, of course, is not the type of man to do a lot of wild sweeping simply to give the dramatic impression of being a new broom. He can be relied upon to try to retain a few of Byrnes' able departmental counselors at least until he familiarizes himself with the details of operations under way. But he also is an ideal choice to make certain that our attempts to reach an understanding with the Russians are not sabotaged by the inability of the State and War departments to work together.

Once we have begun to carry out a fixed policy with firm will and unified effort, neither appeasing nor getting tough, but simply doing unto others as they do unto us, the time has come for a positive step forward in the waging of peace. This step is obvious, but the execution of it is enormously difficult. It is to inform ourselves as thoroughly as we can about Russia and the Russians—what they are doing, thinking, fearing and hoping—and, in turn, to inform the Russians all about us and our intentions. By learning all we can about the Russians and their state of mind, we can ourselves determine whether our fear of eventual attack from them is justified. We know that their fear of attack from us is not justified, and if we are diligent and persevering enough in a prolonged effort, it is just possible that we can convince today's rulers of Russia, or their successors, that a peaceful solution of some permanence can evolve.

If we are to acquire genuine knowledge about the Russian state of mind, to understand why they do some of the things that seem incomprehensible to us, it is necessary for us to try to put ourselves in their position, to see them as they see themselves, and to see ourselves as they see us. In this little volume Edgar Snow presents interesting and provocative material designed to contribute to that purpose. While I do not agree with all of Mr. Snow's conclusions and proposals, particularly those in Chapter IV of this book, I believe his challenging ideas should have the widest possible reading by Americans. Based on years of close and searching examination of the Russian point of view, some of the revelations will outrage Americans accustomed to seeing Russians as they choose to see them, and ourselves as we like to see ourselves. But they constitute a contribution to an understanding of the world's most explosive problem today, and serve a useful purpose in the business of waging peace.

To inform the Russians about us in the process of waging peace is the toughest problem of all. When Hitler and Hirohito and Mussolini were still going strong, President Roosevelt said: "The Soviet Union, as everybody who has the courage to face the facts knows, is run by a dictatorship as absolute as any other dictatorship in the world today." That is at least as true today as it was then. And there is abundant evidence that this dictatorship is convinced that eventual war between communism and our form of democracy for the domination of the world is inevitable, in spite of all the fine words to the contrary. This dictatorship, as has been so often demonstrated, simply will not allow us to get our story across to the Russian people, because of its censorship of all information from foreign sources. The best we can do at present is to repeat and repeat and again repeat our story to the representatives of the dictatorship who are permitted to hear it, and to strive in every way possible to bring about a change which will permit us to enjoy a wider circulation of it at some future date.

The current prospect of changing the minds of those who rule Russia through the Politburo is not

bright. But there is some hope. Mr. Victor A. Kravchenko, who ought to know, has stated that even when
Stalin passes on, his successor is certain to be just as
hell bent on war with us as Mr. Kravchenko considers
the Generalissimo to be. The fact remains that Mr.
Kravchenko himself not very long ago was a Communist Party wheelhorse and he changed his mind
after he had the opportunity of observing the way
a western capitalistic society operates, and convinc-
ing himself that this was the true democratic way
of life.

Even if the men now ruling Russia do not change
their ideas, there is the very definite possibility that
the physical identities of the rulers will change. That
Generalissimo Stalin and his intimate associates live
in fear of this has been demonstrated again and
again by their own acts. Better than anybody else,
they know how many of the Russian leaders in high
places deserted communism during the war, and
how many have since renounced the Party and fled for
their lives, after converting themselves to a belief in
democracy, according to the Western definition of
that term. Ironically, while the American soldiers
were not supposed to know what they were fighting
for, and the Russian soldiers were supposed to understand completely, Russian soldiers and high-ranking

officers sometimes deserted their cause *en masse,* while desertions from the American forces were so negligible as to be practically nonexistent.

The fact is, the question of whether or not the U.S.S.R. has a machinery for the continuity of government that will function under the human stress of the individual lust for power of its rulers is one of the many great imponderables in the problem of waging peace with the Russians.

When you are dealing with imponderables, you must play the whole field of possibilities, and in so doing bring every shred of information you can gather to bear on them. This is the acrobatic assignment to which we Americans are committed. Since information is the business of the press and radio, the press and radio today play a more important role in waging peace than ever before in history —more important, because if we fail to accomplish this mission, then humanity faces extermination.

(1)
WHY WE DON'T UNDERSTAND THE RUSSIANS

IN PEKING, just before the invasion of China in 1937, a Japanese army spokesman used to lecture us about the "misbehavior" of the Chinese, whom he continually exhorted to "adopt a sincere attitude" toward Japan. One day a correspondent asked the colonel to tell us exactly what he meant by a sincere attitude. Nothing loath, and with a perfectly dead-pan face, he replied, "Sincere Chinese should be humble and obedient."

At the time we all thought that merely amusing, but in retrospect I realized that the Japanese had been quite in earnest. His whole feudal training and discipline as a soldier and lowly subject of the Emperor had taught him that an inferior in rank and power must practice humility and obedience to those above him. China was in such a position with regard to Japan and should behave accordingly; otherwise she was insincere.

It was a trivial incident but there were many more like it. If we had taken closer note of the meaning of words as Japanese used them in still earlier days, we might have been able to persuade them to live in peace with the world.

Differences in words and word-values underlie much of our misunderstanding of other countries, and today this applies with special force in the case of Russia. We may some day have one language in use everywhere, but meanwhile, if we are to have one world, we should at least have one political lexicon with a few accepted definitions for the simplest words. Even when Russian speeches are accurately translated our statesmen, press and public often do not know what these "freedom-loving allies" are talking about. Words connote one thing against a unique background of Russian history, language, culture and Marxist ideology superimposed on Tsarist atavisms. They often mean something else when put into an English language enriched through centuries of growth of institutions, thought and experience not duplicated in Russia.

Only scientists, musicians, and chess-players can as yet speak across the continents with exact comprehension of each other's moves and methods; political man lacks definitions of even the basic concepts written into our international formulae for the exigent tomorrow. Yet a fair margin of agreement on meanings is not unattainable, if we make the effort. In the long run it is the end purpose toward which all meetings and conferences with the Russians have been aimed, from Moscow to Teheran, to the Waldorf-Astoria and back to Moscow again. Without a minimum vocabulary in common we shall fail.

Conflicts of meanings exist in the United Nations charter itself, as well as in speeches delivered under its auspices. Take the expression "human rights," for which a definition was actually sought in San Francisco. The Russians wanted "the right to work" included, which was frowned upon by some, and both the British and Russians opposed the American wish to include "the right to free enterprise"; both also grew perplexed when it was proposed to bring in practically the whole Bill of Rights. The search was quickly abandoned for the sake of expediency, but it was probably a mistake; it is doubtful if anything more fundamental has been tackled by the UN since then.

In Paris and London and New York, Messrs. Molotov, Bevin and Byrnes used the same words over and over again, and since they never defined them the speakers seemed to be saying approximately the same things. But they often concluded in acrimonious debate, each suspecting the other of "insincerity." Speaking of his interviews with Soviet diplomats Ernest Bevin, a labor boss but no Marxist, has said repeatedly, "I can't understand them," and "I don't understand." Back from Paris, and reporting to Congress, Senator Vandenberg frankly admitted a mutual unintelligibility between Russia and the United States.

"For example, they certainly could not agree," he said, "on a definition of 'democracy,' although this is the objective both profess."

After quitting his post as ambassador to Russia, Averell Harriman accused the Russians of violating certain terms, "as we understand them," of armistices made in Eastern Europe. Yet Harriman himself went over every word in those agreements. The explanation seems to be that he and Sir Archibald Clark-Kerr simply signed them without realizing their implicit authorization of Red Army measures to which we later had to raise objections.

Molotov may have been technically correct when he said, "Everybody who can read and write can understand the Soviet Union," but in fact the significance of his lectures often escapes most Americans because he constantly invokes references to doctrines unknown by his listeners. One fundamental trouble is that in America we have no political theory, but many theories in competition and flux. We are "polytheorists," which means that we have no state dogma except in ambiguous terms, while the Russians have one state theory which imposes unanimity of thought, an accepted system of semantics, a political folklore understood by all.

2

STRESSING the urgent "need for a definition of liberty," Abraham Lincoln observed in 1864:

"We all declare for liberty but we do not mean the same thing. With some the word liberty may mean for each man to do as he pleases with himself and the product of his labor; while with others the same word may mean for some men to do as they please with other men and the product of other men's labor. Here are two incompatible things called by the same name, liberty." We still lack a universal definition of liberty as well as a host of other words.

Vandenberg complained that he could not agree with the Russians on the meaning of "democracy," but it is doubtful whether Congress would be able to agree either, and Vandenberg did not tell us exactly what he himself had in mind. On the other hand, there is no reason why senators should not know what the Stalinist believes. They can refer to the official Soviet Political Dictionary and find the word neatly packaged for them.

I hope no one gets the idea that this discussion advocates a blanket acceptance of Soviet definitions or wholesale approval of Soviet practices. Because the Marxist lexicon differs from Webster is no justification for abuses which occurred under Red Army occupation, such as denials of certain freedoms guaranteed by Yalta to the ex-enemy states. Arrest and imprisonment without charges of recognized due processes of law, and the revival of concentration camps for political prisoners, are obviously not regarded as legitimate even by the Russians themselves, otherwise there would be no necessity for elaborate secrecy and denials of NKVD methods of terror.

But definitions did directly affect many of our disputes over the justification of Soviet punitive techniques and over application of measures in Eastern Europe, particularly in the Balkans, which were provided for in the armistices. My main point here is simply that if the Russians did not observe ethics to which we try to adhere, part of the fault lay with our own lack of concise thinking, our diplomats' belated realization that the words employed meant one thing to the Russians and another to us, and hence their failure to work out compromises in concrete terminology at the time agreements were written.

Take the word "collaborator," employed again and again. Our representatives never defined it and never seriously examined Soviet definitions in theory and practice. In the case of the Philippines also President Roosevelt specifically authorized punishment of collaborators, yet when it came to application the Filipino officials were given no workable formula. Former President Osmena told me that despite repeated efforts with the administration, Congress and the Army, he never could get an official meaning adopted and thus on his return to Manila he was never able to act effectively against outstanding Filipinos who had worked for the Japanese.

Similarly, although we fought a war against "the fascists," and exchanged the word in congratulatory speech after speech with our allies, Congress never attempted to define this enemy that cost us so much blood and treasure. It is a safe bet that no two men in Truman's Cabinet would give the same definition of fascism today. The only thing certain is that all of them would reject the following answer, as supplied by the Soviet official sources:

"*Fascism*: One of the forms of open bourgeois dictatorship, arising in Italy after the first imperialist war, and in several capitalist countries, during a general crisis in capitalism." Likewise for another, still in common use: "a manifestation of monopoly capitalism in its most imperialistic phase."

Those two sentences contain four Marxist terms each of which has a long history and technology behind it. Judging from my own conversations with our generals, congressmen and diplomats, they are quite unfamiliar with such terminology, which they dismiss with contempt as "communist jargon," but they assuredly disagree with the general idea, that fascism is a specific disease of capitalism. Quite the contrary. Most of them pretty generally inform me that there is no essential difference between fascism and the Soviet system. They reason that both are dictatorships, both use similar methods; ergo, they are the same thing.

Such men would be astounded to learn that Russians believe that we also live under a form of

46

dictatorship. Theory teaches them that fascism is a form of capitalism. "The American way" is a form of capitalism. All capitalist societies are dominated by the bourgeoisie. And "the forms of bourgeois states are extremely varied," wrote Lenin, "but in essence they are all the same: in one way or another, in final analysis, all these states are inevitably the dictatorship of the bourgeoisie."

Thus when Molotov and Vyshinsky and such people spit out common words like fascism, imperialism, feudalism, dictatorship, or collaborator, and purr over favorites like socialism, democracy and communism, they are not only talking in Russian but simultaneously using a second language which is rarely translated for the American newspaper reader. They are speaking in "Marxian," derived directly from accepted political scripture replete with precise "scientific" phraseology. They know that everything they say will be checked, compared, interpreted and annotated by the Red professors, and that they must be prepared to reconcile their utterances with classical doctrine. They are often less concerned that their Anglo-American colleagues should understand them than they are that they should not be misunderstood by the magistrates at home.

47

3

Consider Molotov's precondition for a treaty with Germany, his reiteration that we must first clean up "remnants of German fascism." To Americans that may be just a phrase which has become a nauseous cliché. But Soviet diplomats must deal in clichés; variations might be misinterpreted in Moscow. A whole volume could be filled with the evolution of the phrase mentioned and with official commentaries, from Stalin down. To any Russian Marxist it means, in brief: liquidation of the Prussian Junkers and the landlord system throughout Germany, distribution of land to the peasants, an end to the economic power of large and middle capitalists, state ownership of important industry, suppression of anti-Soviet elements, and a German regime observing policies of economic, political and military friendship and collaboration with the U.S.S.R.

It doesn't necessarily follow that Moscow may not settle for less, but all the foregoing intention is implicit whenever Molotov demands "eradication of the remnants of German fascism." Probably no such disturbing picture crosses the minds of Gen-

48

eral Marshall and Harry Truman, if and when they use the term.

In 1945 Molotov made the following statement on foreign policy: "The Soviet Union has always given first place to promoting universal peace and the development of international business relations. While we are living in a 'system of states' and while the roots of fascism and imperialist aggression have not been finally extirpated, our vigilance in regard to possible new violators of peace should not slacken, and concern for the strengthening of co-operation between peace-loving powers will continue to be our utmost duty."

Read "as we understand it," that is but a simple expression of desire to co-operate with the United States and other democratic powers. But here "system of states" is a key phrase, and it refers of course to a famous dictum of Lenin. He warned that while the Soviet Union existed in a complex "system of states" of which only one was socialist, capitalist encirclement and bloody battles were inevitable. Thus Molotov, while holding out the olive branch to the capitalist states, keeps himself on the record as an orthodox Leninist. He also notifies Marxists to be on guard and that alliances and power politics are still the order of the day.

49

On the other hand, we often get unduly irritated through misconception of the real targets of Soviet irony. If *Pravda* denounces "warmongers among the ruling circles" of the United States it is not directly attacking Truman and his cabinet; it means the entire complex of capitalist forces which it imagines really decide policy. When Molotov bitterly contrasted Russia's terrible losses with "American riches" made from the war, Mr. Byrnes bridled at a fancied personal insult. But Molotov was not impugning Byrnes or the honor of Americans as a whole. He was talking about the 35 billion dollars in new profits created in war industry and about the "monopoly capitalists" who, his informants tell him, now hold most of it.

Although our diplomats and State Department officials assigned to Russian matters should normally gather in such recondite meanings and evaluate them it is probably too much to expect "everybody who can read and write" to detect them. But there is considerably less excuse for our mass ignorance about elementary facts concerning Russia, if public opinion is to play an intelligent role in determining policy toward our gravest problem in foreign affairs.

4

ACCORDING to a survey made by Princeton University, in our adult population of about 90,000,000, there are 63,000,000 of us who think that "abolition of private ownership" in Russia means that all goods are held in common. Two out of three Americans don't know that Russians can privately own homes, furniture, cars, etc., and that farmers till individual plots. The same inquiry disclosed that about 64% of adult Americans don't know that wages are not equal in Russia but differential; 83% don't know that most Russians are *not* members of the Communist Party. Seven out of nine Americans don't know that Russia produced most of the war materials used by the Red Army and only one out of two knows that the avowed aim of the Soviet government is to build Russia into a socialist state. Thirty-eight million Americans of voting age "don't know at all what kind of government Russia has."

Much can be blamed on Moscow's own censorship and absurd secrecy and on an incredibly blockheaded treatment of American correspondents—perhaps the one truly incomprehensible fact about Russia. But that is no justification for our mental darkness about the only country Americans profess to fear today. Such elementary things could be learned in ten minutes spent in any library.

The Princeton poll did not ask the question, Is the Soviet system called communism or socialism? but probably not one American in ten could explain the difference. If you look into Webster's Collegiate Dictionary you will see "socialist" defined as a *synonym* of "collectivist, nihilist, communist, anarchist, bolshevik," all listed together on the naive premise that "these groups are agreed in distrusting capitalist control of industry." It may be possible to achieve greater confusion in one syllogism but personally I have not actually seen it demonstrated.

Yet lexicographers can hardly be blamed for our own political illiteracy. They are supposed to inscribe meanings in common American usage and there is no doubt the above definition reflects it. You don't have to go into a classroom to hear similar misconstructions. You need only read the papers or listen to the speeches of American congressmen, senators and statesmen, whose daily crimes against political semantics are a national disgrace.

It is not required that we "accept" Marxism in order to study its terms, any more than you need believe your distant ancestor was a gorilla in order to study Darwin's theory and understand it. But some people are smugly satisfied to dismiss both Marx and Darwin as "foreign propagandists." Unfortunately, they predominate in the lunatic fringe that raves about preventive war, and bringing Russia to reason by dropping A-bombs on Moscow.

Some may say, "Let them understand us, why should we try to understand them?" It is a poor answer from anyone who wants to fight Russia. He should hope the contrary, that the Russians are more ignorant of our problems than we are of theirs. Woe to him who goes to war without knowing his enemy, as Hitler learned, and definitely it is not possible to know Russia while believing that nihilist is a synonym for socialist. The unfortunate fact is, Soviet citizens are obliged to make a far more detailed study of capitalism than ours make of socialism.

It so happens that Marxism and Soviet ideology are not passing notions, as many thought before Hitler's defeat, but living forces which grip the

53

minds of increasing millions of men and women with whom we share the world. "Marxian" is a language we must learn, sooner or later, if only to define our differences with Russia and leftist Europe and Asia in terms of agreements we uphold in common.

No doubt the task of understanding is enormously complicated by the fact that Moscow speaks with two voices. One is the language of Soviet nationalism, slowly integrating itself within the deep forces of Russian history. The other is still the language of social revolution. Every Soviet leader is in a sense a dual personality: first a Russian nationalist, a practical politician concerned with immediate problems of security and power; second, a Marxist, a socialist, an adherent of theoretical doctrines. This dualism was long personified by the Soviet government's efforts to maintain collaboration with capitalist states and at the same time to give haven to a Comintern pledged to overthrow them. And because Marxism-Leninism remains the guiding philosophy behind Soviet domestic policy, outside politicians and observers (including American Communists) continue to confuse the vital interests of Russia as a state and going concern with what are often purely theoretical abstractions or propaganda aims.

Soviet representatives at home and abroad more often speak as pure nationalists than as Marxists, but always as something of both. Now they may adopt a position solely for tactical reasons, again for long-range strategic ends; sometimes a speech is worded in Marxist stereotypes purely to satisfy the record, sometimes in earnest and as a guide to incipient action; in some situations they are bluffing in the ancient ways of power politics, to make the best of a bad bargain; in others, vital national interests and theoretical aims are identical.

Few foreign communists understand this inter-play of nationalist and socialist forces in Soviet policy. With their overemphasis on the doctrines of socialist power and their lack of experience in the functions and responsibilities of national power, American communists frequently get them-selves badly mangled between the main gears and the auxiliary wheels of Soviet diplomacy. Thus it happens repeatedly that they lead their followers into political cul-de-sacs because of their over-zealous haste to march in behind what they mistake for the main Soviet column, only to find themselves isolated and forced to beat a hasty retreat when events reveal that they were supporting a mere feint or parry while the principal aims of Soviet strategy lay elsewhere. Russians are often as amazed at such behavior as we are.

All Soviet pronouncements really should be read with bi-focal lenses. It is necessary to know Russia as a functioning nation, its real physical possibilities and limitations, as well as the fount of Marxist dogma, and what is discarded theory and what is living practice. A little study and Russia is no riddle. It is easier for us than it is for Russians to understand America, because there is a Rosetta Stone to Soviet politics. Without it, you may well end up with Hitler.

Unfortunately, instead of seeking out the services of men with a sense of history who have made an objective effort to understand Russia in relation to the world political complex, the tendency in government now is to depend upon sentinels whose training has best equipped them to live in a state of maximum political obfuscation. Everyone knows that since Roosevelt's death our foreign policy has more and more been determined by generals and admirals on the basis of what they see as "strategic necessities" in a hypothetical war with Russia. This might not be bad if these gentlemen had somehow acquired a political education since leaving West Point, but such is not always the case.

I cannot forget having asked one such general what he had learned, after he had spent two years as military attache in Moscow, and his considered reply, "Russia has nothing to teach us—nothing except perhaps the use of aircraft under winter conditions." Philip Famyonville, the only general in our army who was a real scholar of Russian as well as Soviet history, understood both languages used by Moscow, and was the only officer in the combined Anglo-American staffs to predict correctly the course of the Soviet-German war, has been rewarded by demotion and an obscure job in the Ordnance branch. Preoccupied with plans for hypothetical war, the armed services are often dominated by men who understand least about the political terms—and hence about the political consequences—of modern war.

5

During the last war our ignorance of Soviet vocabulary led to countless misunderstandings, and it still does today. Take General Patrick Hurley's celebrated interview with Stalin, in the spring of 1945. Hurley had come to the conclusion (against the facts and opinion of experienced foreign service officers) that the Chinese Communists were being supported by Russia, that they could not stand without Russian aid; in short, Stalin was running them. Hurley thought that if he could get Stalin to agree to withdraw his hand then he could fix up a deal to liquidate the "Communist problem." Accordingly, he went to the Kremlin and in the course of exchanging pleasantries he asked Stalin what he would "settle for" in China. Stalin replied in time-worn phrases that "the Soviet Government was determined not to interfere in the internal affairs of China," but said that he would like to see the Communists enter a coalition government with the nationalists under Chiang Kai-shek, whom he recognized to be head of the legal Chinese Government.

Hurley apparently interpreted Stalin's remarks as an "undertaking" that Moscow would repudiate the Communists if they did not come to terms with the Kuomintang, and he wired the White House that he and Uncle Joe were in complete agreement. Our Moscow embassy understood Stalin's language in this case, however. Men present at the interview told me they had, after reading Hurley's extravagant claims, hastily informed the State Department that he was under serious misapprehensions. Nevertheless, back in Chungking, General Hurley continued to assure Truman that he had the Chinese Communists in his pocket—till political explosions after V-J Day demonstrated they were anywhere else but.

Another example of Soviet-American misunderstanding over China arose when the Soviet-Chinese treaty of alliance was signed in August, 1946. The Chinese envoy, T. V. Soong, consulted with our diplomats in Moscow, as the treaty was more Roosevelt's idea than Chiang Kai-shek's. Americans okayed every phrase in it. In the end our mission in Moscow seemed satisfied that this document would somehow demolish the Chinese Communists. One of our generals (an astute soldier) who had advised Soong during negotiations told me quite flatly that we had got a treaty which would commit the Russians to exclude Chinese Red forces from Manchuria, and not to render them any aid. "It will mean the end of the Chinese Communists," he said.

When the treaty finally was published, however, it not only contained nothing that could be called a repudiation of Mao Tsê-tung's following, but included at least two clauses which, if read "as Russians understand them," would enable them legally to deal with Chinese troops other than Chiang Kai-shek's, and even to co-operate with them "against the enemy." Our people apparently skipped this small print, but fortunately the Russians have not taken full advantage of that negligence.

Woolly thinking also prevailed during the writing of armistice agreements with Rumania, Bulgaria and other satellite states. The Rumanian armistice obligated any post-defeat government to abolish all pro-Hitler organizations, "as well as other organizations conducting propaganda hostile to the United Nations, *in particular to the Soviet Union*," and to prohibit "the existence" of such activities for all time. Control of all forms of public expression was placed under "the Allied (Soviet) High Command" and the government undertook to "carry out all its instructions and orders." Yet at no time was the phrase "Allied (Soviet) High Command" defined, nor was Anglo-American responsibility. Lacking that, the clear implication was unlimited power of decision to the Red Army.

Much the same terms appeared in armistices for

Bulgaria and Hungary. In addition, all shipping belonging to Bulgaria was to be turned over to Russia, as well as control of industry and transport. All war matériel, defined as "equipment belonging to, used by, or intended for use by, enemy military or para-military formations or members thereof" was devised to the Red Army in each case. Considering the nature of the *carte blanche* we thus sanctioned, it is perhaps surprising that any opposition to Communist Party rule in Balkan countries was permitted at all.

Of course the Russians knew perfectly well, in that case, that the Allied powers had no intention of underwriting communism in the Balkans. But in fairness we must ask ourselves *why*, from the Soviet viewpoint, things should always be read in *our* way. Russian and English are official languages on a parity, but behind them both lie philosophies also implicitly accepted on a plane of equality. People living on their one-sixth of the earth have been taught to think and act inside a pattern of their own for over a quarter of a century now and they take it about as much for granted as we do ours. When they made agreements covering enemy countries they did so because the terms seemed workable within a projection of meanings familiar

61

to them. Our generals and politicians never assumed
that any allied agreement required us to sponsor
communist parties in our occupied areas. Why
should the Russians have assumed the same agreements required them to support capitalist parties
in theirs?

Yet much hysteria about Russia originates in
such assumptions. Of course it is silly to look for
objectivity in matters of serious political struggle,
and it is no more to be expected in certain sections
of our press than it is in *Red Star* or *Izvestia*. But
while it may be all right to fool the other fellow,
there is some danger that we may be deceived by
our own propaganda. No doubt the Russians have
tried to prevent us from looking behind their iron
curtain, but there is also evidence that a smoke
screen of our own making sometimes keeps us from
looking out.

It was not the iron curtain, for example, that
prevented the American people from understanding
the significance of Stalin's speech in February,
1946, or his interview with Alexander Werth. Both
were widely misinterpreted in the American press,
as well as misread by generals and diplomats.

Here it was chiefly noted that Stalin said the
war had arisen as "the inevitable result" of the

development of rivalries "on the basis of monopoly capitalism" and implied that it had been impossible to avoid war in a capitalist world. He called for "a new, mighty upsurge in national economy" in the U.S.S.R., stressing heavy industry especially. It was noted that Stalin barely mentioned allied contributions to victory and made no promises for the new-born UN. On such grounds the majority of commentators concluded that the speech was bellicose, menacing, uncompromising, showed Russian insincerity, and revealed deep plotting to bolshevize us in a future war.

That was perhaps an expected reaction from permanently conditioned Russophobes, of whom we have as many as the Russians have xenophobes. But even sober and normally cautious prophets drew strange conclusions. For a sampler, here is Walter Lippmann: "Stalin has made the decision to make military power his first objective," he sonorously intoned, "and we are forced to make a corresponding decision." Solemnly he warned his very influential following that, "Since Russia is going to organize 'a new mighty upsurge' of *power for military ends*," we must make haste with the atomizers.

With all due respect—which is considerable—

63

to Mr. Lippmann, there is no word for such logic
but asinine. Stalin had actually said nothing about
industrializing to assert military power or conquest but had stressed the heavy war damage inflicted on Russia and the need for reconstruction.
Demaree Bess has reported talking to a diplomat
just back from Moscow who excitedly told him
Russia was feverishly preparing for war. Asked
to explain, the diplomat had no testimony to offer
except Soviet emphasis on increased steel production. To Bess, as to anyone else who has studied
Soviet planning over the past two decades, this
thinker was just funny.

6

So it is worth cursorily re-examining Stalin's
speech because it still dramatically illustrates why
we often misunderstand Russia.

Remember that it was the first comprehensive
post-war review by the head of the state. It was
an election speech, addressed to Russian voters,
not to our Congress. Though everyone knew the
result in advance, still the party was up for judg-
ment by the people and the purpose was to paint
the best possible picture of its achievements. Trib-

utes to lend-lease would have been as much out of place as hosannas to the Red Army in Governor Dewey's campaign. Finally, such an important pronouncement was not just the personal expression of an individual but a synthesis of views within the Central Committee that rules Russia, representing a reconciliation of practical and theoretical differences bound to exist. Probably every word was thoroughly discussed in the Politburo before it was approved.

Now, everybody who has followed Soviet politics knows that the evolution of the war and its outcome presented Marxist theorists with thorny new questions which have never been answered in a finished thesis. In a later article I hope to explore some of these questions in detail, but here it must suffice to point to the outstanding fact that the "imperialist states" did not perform as prophesied. The "world bourgeoisie" rejected their one great opportunity to unite and destroy the one and only socialist state. Instead, the socialist fatherland was saved from destruction by an alliance that endured with the most advanced capitalist powers of the earth.

Until this conflict Marxist speculation had always assumed that in the event of an "imperialist war" (struggle for redivision of the earth) against the Soviet Union, proletarian uprisings would occur in major capitalist countries and Russia would be saved by a combination of her own fighting strength plus insurrections in the rear of the enemy. This idea is organic with Leninism and traces also to a basic Marxist theory of "the breakdown of capitalism"—when conditions become intolerable for the working class it rises and takes power.

In the early days of Soviet-Nazi war the Red Army soldiers were still so imbued with the concept of working-class solidarity that thousands were captured because they were reluctant to shoot Germans. Up till then it had been called an "imperialist war" and the soldiers believed there would soon be revolutions. Why kill future comrades? In consternation the Politburo then ordered intensified nationalistic indoctrination in the Red Army and raised the slogan of the "patriotic war."

Not only were there no proletarian revolts of the classical pattern in Germany or Japan, but the socialist union was saved by a combination of its own fighting strength and the social and political stability of its "imperialistic" allies—which also raised the novel question of socialists dying to preserve capitalist states. During the war I asked General A. A. Scherbakov, then head of the Red Army political department, and a member of the Politburo, whether the fact that the greatest capitalist power had come to the aid of socialist Russia did not introduce an entirely new stage in world history, one quite unforeseen by Lenin's classic *The Imperialist War.* He readily agreed that it did; things had happened which Lenin could not anticipate.

Other theses were shaken. American capitalism was no longer considered near the "breakdown" stage. Some men in the party thought that, in various forms, it might last another half-century.

Did this new situation demand a formal revision in one set of doctrines? Should it be quietly laid to rest, along with Marx's prophecy of "the withering away of the state" under socialism? Was the corollary a new orientation of Soviet policy based on an assumption of peaceful co-existence of the "two systems" for a long time? Widespread debate and discussion ensued within the party, but Stalin's speech was the nearest thing to an answer publicly to emerge from the secret controversy.

Stalin handled the whole question by implication and in compromise. Paying homage to dogma by attributing the origins of the war to irreconcilable contradictions within the capitalist system, he also acknowledged an entirely new development.

"The second world war," he said, "differed fundamentally from the first in character." Abandoning altogether Moscow's earlier thesis that before 1941 the conflict was an "imperialist war," Stalin said that "unlike the first world war, *from the very outset* it assumed the character of an anti-fascist war, a war of liberation, one of whose aims was the restoration of democratic liberties."

From a theoretical standpoint this admission was vastly significant. If it was possible for capitalist nations to fight an anti-fascist war, a war for democratic liberties, before Soviet participation as well as afterward, then peaceful collaboration for the same ends is clearly possible. It is from this thesis that Molotov's November statement before the UN derives its authority:

"The war vividly demonstrated that states with widely different political structure (i.e., imperialist and socialist) had extremely important interests in common. Mutual aid between them produced great results. The recognition (by the Soviet Union) of the principles of such international co-operation *has a profound meaning*. It reflects the firm will to achieve universal peace and readiness to enter into peaceful competition . . . between states and social systems."

Another overlooked point in Stalin's speech was from a practical viewpoint more important than the first. The Soviet Union hopes, he said, eventually to produce 60 million tons of steel annually. *Only then*, he added, could the homeland be considered "guaranteed against all possible eventualities"—i. e., wars. But "that will take three more five-year plans, if not more." In other words, by the hardest kind of toil, Russia aspires to make, in 1961, two-thirds as much steel as the present capacity of the United States. Stalin would be 82 by then. But he probably does not expect to live long enough to see Russia guaranteed against all eventualities—and hence not long enough to be able to launch an aggressive war against the United States, even if he so desired. Think it over.

Official pronouncement from the Kremlin, Alexander Werth's interview, and Soviet initiative in disarmament proposals, further confirm such interpretations—as I shall attempt to show later on. Here I only wish to urge that we learn to read the Soviet languages before we draw conclusions of despair. It isn't a question of doing it to please the Russians but to keep our own blood pressure down. Molotov's bluntness, Vyshinsky's sarcasms, Gromyko's dour lack of humor, can all be a source of enlightenment or quiet amusement, if we know what they really mean. And it only tickles them to get your goat, just as it pleases Uncle Joe to egg them on to do all the bluffing and bargaining abroad, while he confines himself to rare utterances from the Kremlin, of calm logic and fact.

Meanwhile, don't be too exercised over the septic exchanges of opinion of various conferences and UN sessions. Look upon them as post-graduate courses for diplomats who gave up their home work too soon. It is a fine thing to compel them to sit and listen to each other over and over again; some ideas may eventually penetrate. If Soviet Russians won't learn anything about our point of view, we may learn something about theirs and be so much the richer. Someone may even suggest that Russian be made a compulsory study in our primary schools, as English now is in Russia.

Personally, I fully agreed with Admiral Nimitz when he said he "wasn't the slightest bit distressed" over all the harsh words being thrown around in the conferences. "It took the colonies thirteen years to agree on a constitution, and they all spoke the same language," he wisely observed. If we keep at it we may eventually get at least thirteen definitions in common. Armed with that dictionary Truman could get together with Stalin and agree on plans for some good, solid two-way streets.

----

[2]

AS IT LOOKS
TO
IVAN IVANOVITCH

WHEN I first went to Russia I had a translator for a while whom I used to call Three-in-One, though she never knew why. Everything in Russia was always dandy for Galya, but if sudden changes were made they were dandy too. She saw no evil, spoke no evil, heard no evil. She was monotonous company but an excellent translator. One day I played rather an unkind trick on her.

Late the night before, the Foreign Office had issued a special press communique announcing that the title Marshal of the Soviet Union had been conferred on Comrade Stalin. We were going to visit a school early in the morning and when we started out I knew that Three-in-One hadn't seen the papers, which didn't appear till around ten. I asked her how it was that Stalin could be supreme c-in-c and head of the defense council, when he wasn't a marshal, nor even a general. How could a mere party secretary command an army of 20 million men?

"You don't understand," explained Galya. "Stalin's position is unique and he needs no titles.

If he became a marshal it would put him on the
same plane with the others." She gave all the reasons why he should remain a plain tovarisch and
privately I agreed with them. But on our way
home we came upon a wall newspaper and there
was the half-page picture of Stalin with the announcement. Galya was dumfounded, but not for
long. "Of course as supreme Commander-in-Chief
and Chairman of the Defense Council," she
beamed, "he had to become a marshal. It's necessary to maintain discipline."

Three-in-One was always shocked that I wouldn't
accept at face value all that Moscow newspapers
had to say. If I criticized it was because I was an
"imperialist." I was the first foreigner she had
worked for but when I went away she did transla-
tions for other correspondents. The next year I
returned and met her again and she told me she
had learned to understand Americans.

"Now I know you don't mean any harm," she
said. "You just like to criticize because you think
nobody is perfect."

"That's right," I told her, "you've got the idea
at last."

Of course there are Russians who disbelieve
everything they read in Soviet papers, but there

is no more open-mindedness in their heresy than there is in Galya's faith. The liberal has never thrived in Russia. Catherine the Great used to correspond with Voltaire but neither she nor the Tsars, no more than the Soviets today, followed him when he avowed, "I disagree with everything you say, but I will defend with my life your right to say it."

A year in Moscow, and a daily diet of papers that never express but one point of view, develops in most Americans a pathological need for a pulpit, even when they agree with 80% of what they read. After being deprived of his right to criticize for months even the most amiable correspondent rebels by spilling a wholesale accumulation of grievances as soon as he is back on American soil.

Soviet censors for months successfully deprive somebody like Brooks Atkinson of his right to disagree, but when he leaves Russia he goes straight to the front page of the *Times*, to unload all his animadversions in one series of articles which makes *Pravda* scream "pen bandit!" at him. Maybe his criticisms taken by themselves were not a balanced picture of Russia, but if read with his year's reporting from Moscow they are. The trouble is, nobody, not even *Pravda* editors, re-reads a year's old newspapers. If Atkinson had been allowed to space out his subjective comments in his objective dispatches from Moscow, then his readers would have gotten a steady diet of honest American reporting, on the whole sympathetic, of Russia and her problems. Instead, they got a single concentration of bile which led thousands of Americans to misunderstand both Atkinson and Russia. This happens again and again, but the Russians never see how their censorship defeats itself.

Knowing Atkinson, I'm sure he would have preferred to enter his complaints against the Soviet system in Moscow's own press, and heard the case argued on the spot, but that was quite impossible. I am also sure that after being home for six months he would not write his findings in the same way.

Under such conditions those of us who were in Moscow during the war tended to idealize the American press and the American mind and to attribute unparalleled objectivity to it. Coming home, after four years of war reporting all over the world, was disillusioning. We found almost as much chauvinism in our press as in the Soviet, and about as little attempt to understand the other fellow's point of view. And we got just as tired of always being shown only the buffalo on the nickel as seeing only the Red Indian head on the other side.

It isn't as exclusively America the Just in our press as it is Russia the Just over there; I wouldn't be publishing this here if it were. But it is far too much that way for comfort. I don't like dictator- ships and I wouldn't like to spend my life under the Russian system. The Soviet state of today is a product of Marxism, imposed on a long tradition of Tsarist absolutism, the inevitable outgrowth of a history different from our own, and it is no more possible nor desirable to transplant a copy of that system to this country than it is for us to repudiate our whole past. But Russia is a great nation and has certain vital interests which would be the same under any regime. We cannot ignore those interests merely because we dislike or don't understand Soviet communism. For a year now grown-up folks have been busily playing a game called What's behind the Iron Curtain, while pay- ing little attention to what's in front of it or attempting to see ourselves as others see us.

We are not at war nor anywhere near it and in peacetime there is no excuse for a democracy wear- ing blinders in its own house. Self-criticism is food for the soul of freedom. Goethe was entirely right when he said, "Nothing is more frightful than ignorance in action," and no one is more ignorant than the man for whom the other chap is always wrong.

2

CONCRETELY, we say that the Russians have not observed the Atlantic Charter and that they have violated or sabotaged other agreements. They are opposing the "rest of the world" by their policies in Germany, Austria, Poland, China and elsewhere. They made imperialist demands on Turkey and Iran and encouraged aggressive moves by Yugoslavia and Bulgaria against Greece. Under the guise of "reparations" they established economic monopolies in Eastern Europe against the interests of "free trade." They utilized their occupation to loot Europe and Manchuria, to spread communism, to suppress democracy, and to create satellite regimes.

"Soviet leaders," to sum up a popular view as expressed by Joseph and Stewart Alsop, "have plunged the world into danger and disquiet because they believe that their way of life cannot co-exist with ours."

But how does that look to one "average Russian"

—not the bureaucrat, the Kremlin or the Party zealot?

Before attempting to lift the lid from Ivan Ivanovitch's skull, let me emphasize that this report is not intended to stamp with general approval either Soviet diplomatic or propaganda methods. They are often indefensible even from the standpoint of Soviet interests. Soviet censorship policy, idiotic decisions such as the banning of radio correspondents from Moscow, and similar public-relations techniques, at times seem deliberately calculated to win enemies and antagonize people, and contribute handsomely to Soviet-American misunderstanding.

You are also warned that Ivan gets his foreign news funneled through the propaganda section of the Central Committee of the Communist Party. It is not served in the form of a balanced information diet but consists of items scientifically selected to buttress the main lines of state policy. Soviet foreign policy, as everything else, is not haphazard improvisation but part of dynamic plans with specific objectives. And the press and the foreign news it presents are strictly functional in character.

All that means that Ivan's sources of current knowledge are sharply limited. But the facts presented are usually correct; it is in their selection and emphasis that the reader is led by the nose. Whatever doubts trouble Ivan must grow out of the compulsions of his own inner sense of logic. Admittedly, that is true of many Americans who read but one newspaper; but the difference is that rebuttals, denials, explanations, additional data which might question or contradict, are readily available if Americans want them.

Nevertheless, the average Russian is surprisingly well supplied with surface facts concerning foreign issues; they are indeed an inescapable part of the political indoctrination he receives not only through the press but through instruction in the school, factory, office and club. What Ivan does not know about America's role in the recent war would fill an encyclopedia, but what convictions he does have are tenaciously held and in close agreement with his neighbors. He has got some of the facts but not all of them, and it is in the gaps in his information—which I here assume the reader can supply for himself—that we find the reasons he misunderstands us.

At the outset Ivan's view differs from ours as to the causes of the war and the aims of the peace. Americans tend to assume that things were more or less satisfactory in the world till the rise of the

Axis. Having defeated these disturbers of order the natural aim of man should be to restore the picture as it was. Maybe that suits us, at home, but it doesn't suit Europe, Asia, nor the Russians.

Ivan believes that the war was caused by conflicts within the societies of national states, and because reactionary European capitalism resolved those conflicts by attempting to isolate and destroy the Soviet Union. After crushing his enemies the last thing he expected to see was a return to things as they were.

During the war I had an interesting conversation with a wise European, Zdenek Fierlinger, then Czech ambassador to Moscow and later first socialist premier in Prague. "For Russia," he said, "victory means the opening up of gates which for centuries have barred it from free access to the rest of Europe. Russia will see to it that no force arises again which can form a permanent barrier between the Vistula and the Atlantic Ocean. Far from wanting isolation, the most important conscious hope of victory to the Russian is this new sense of community with Europe."

Invasion of the Soviet Union, as Ivan sees it, was made possible because the Western powers, during and after Versailles, deliberately helped to build up a system of buffer states to block Russia from Europe. He knows that all those states fell in with fascism, when Germany became the pivotal power, to attempt to obliterate Russia. During the war the Germans had allies who helped mobilize behind their invasion the combined resources and man-power of Italy, Austria, Hungary, Rumania, Bulgaria, Greece, Finland, Poland and Czechoslovakia, as well as occupied Western Europe.

3

WHAT, then, did victory mean to the Soviet citizen? It meant that the Red Army had withstood all Europe, excluding Britain. It meant that it was no longer possible for any combination of European powers to think of making war against Russia —without the help of the United States.

Second was the fact that the "ruling class" in states that had voluntarily led their peoples to disaster would be swept into oblivion, along with the political, social, and economic institutions and ideas that had supported them. To the Russians this meant that in the enemy states, certainly in those occupied by the Red Army, the "remnants of feudalism," the broken-down aristocrats, the

privileges of the great land barons, the bureau-
crats, the big capitalists, all the features and personalities of systems that had served fascism, would
be eliminated.

Third, Russians assumed that the world in general would duly understand the momentous political significance of Soviet victory. An entirely new
situation in history was created. Not only had
Russia become the mightiest power in both Europe
and Asia; the socialist movement as a political
force now held the balance of power in the entire
Eurasian complex of states—excluding America,
of course.

Fourth, it was assumed that the world would
now recognize that socialism was a workable form
of society. Whatever else individual Russians
might question in Stalin's speeches, few would deny
that "the Soviet socialist order is stable and capable of enduring." Russians widely believed most
of Europe would also conclude that Soviet victory
proved the superiority of socialism over capitalism.
They believed that capitalism in Europe was led
to its deathbed by its would-be savior—Adolf
Hitler.

Finally, the Russians never forget the frightful
price they paid for demonstrating all that to the

nations—and for their own salvation. They did not attack Germany but were victims of an unprovoked invasion which caused Winston Churchill to exclaim, "No government ever formed among men has been capable of surviving injury so grave and cruel as that inflicted by Hitler on Russia!" Churchill at least was aware that the whole blitz over Britain was a siege of bad weather compared to Russia's ordeal. All Britain's civilian and military dead combined were fewer than the people killed in one Russian city.

At costs which Americans never more than dimly conceived, and have too conveniently obscured, the Russian people, not the atom bomb, cracked the heart of the Wehrmacht before we landed in Europe. More Russians were killed in the Stalingrad campaign alone, while we were still forming an army, than all Americans buried by the war. The Red Army suffered heavier casualties at Kharkov, in a battle most Americans never heard of, than we lost in the entire war against Japan. More than seven million Red Army soldiers were killed by the Germans and their allies, and five to six million civilians. Two dozen Russian soldiers died for every American sacrificed, and about ten died for every allied European soldier—including British,

Canadian, Australian, New Zealand, Indian, Greek, South African, French, Dutch, Danish and Belgian losses. No, the war was not won at Hiroshima, the Russians say. As they see it, if the wall of Russian resistance had collapsed, German scientists might now be studying radio-activity in New York and Washington.

More than 800,000 square miles of Russia were occupied by the Germans and their allies. It was only a tenth of the U.S.S.R. but it held a third of Russia's population and its devastation meant the loss of half the Soviet coal mines, half the electric power, three-fifths of the iron mines, and about half the steel and machinery industry. What the Russians liberated was for the most part a desert of worthless rubble, with its great cities from 30% to 90% destroyed.

Last year Russian authorities told me that four million people in the Ukraine alone would have to live in caves or lean-tos made of wreckage for another two years. Altogether, six million dwellings and buildings, which provided what was very poor housing to 25 million people, were "consumed by fascism," as the Russians say. That is roughly the same thing as losing all the family dwelling units in California, Arkansas, Arizona, Connecticut,

Florida, New Mexico, Oregon, Washington, Vermont, Maine, New Hampshire and Virginia. Imagine another equivalent: that the entire population of New York City, Chicago, Philadelphia, Detroit, Baltimore, Cleveland, St. Louis, Boston, Pittsburgh, Washington, San Francisco, Milwaukee, Buffalo and New Orleans had been rendered homeless by the war.

How many of us would then be worrying about whether the Germans were being told how to vote? Or whether the Rumanians (who massacred over 200,000 Soviet citizens in Odessa alone) were getting "absolutely free elections"? Or whether the Austrians (700,000 volunteered for Der Fuehrer) were losing some of their factories? Or whether the Hungarians (who boasted of killing "a million Russians") had to suffer the pangs of inflation?

Shall we speak seriously of reparations as compensation for Russia's experience? Who can revive her dead? Material damages are estimated at about 200 billion dollars, but it was more than money that went up in smoke. Suppose you had a house (four million *privately owned* dwellings were destroyed in Russia) and now you live in a hole in the earth. What damages do you claim when your child dies of pneumonia? Suppose you had a pair of boots stolen by Fritz and now you must wear straw wrapped round your feet. Is it only the price of the boots you lost?

All that is background to Soviet policies in Europe today. If we entirely ignore it, no bridge to the Russian mind can be found—nor to Yugoslavia, who lost 1,600,000 men out of a population of 17,000,000, nor to Poland, five million of whose inhabitants were killed by the Germans.

Now, the same people who exulted in the light-hearted invasion of Russia—and raised no protest against the looting of tens of thousands of villages, the rape of Russian women, the extermination of six million Jews and political prisoners of all races, the enslavement of millions of captured laborers—have seen a little retaliation. The Russians are taking back some of the tractors and livestock which the Germans stole or destroyed; they are restoring some of their factories with German machines; they are carrying out punitive political and economic measures.

At Potsdam, Russia was allowed six billion dollars in reparations from Germany, which is a fraction of what German citizens gave to their effort to bring their neighbor down in ruin. She had probably taken somewhat more. She also is collecting a total of 800 million dollars in indemnities from Hungary, Rumania and Finland, and another 100 million from Italy. Those levies about equal what British and American taxpayers will, by the end of 1947, have contributed to the support of "our Germans" without a noticeable whimper. Even if the penalties were ten times as heavy they would not today give back to Ivan his house, his boots, a winter coat for his daughter—or, incidentally, his dead sons.

4

Bᴜᴛ we thought Russian demands are extortionate; with abbreviated means of production, some Germans might starve, innocent people may suffer. We pitied the Rumanians and Hungarians. We were anxious to see the Balkan countries returned to normal, and our idea of normal was about the way things were before. As victors who do not know what invasion and fascist barbarism meant to our allies, we were quite prepared to be friends without demanding radical changes in our former foes.

Well, while we were passing out generosity the Russians felt that we and the British owed them a little more sympathy than our ex-enemies. They didn't see why we could not put ourselves in their shoes and see how we liked the holes in them. They heard Ernie Bevin rival Churchill in courting Germany, "and talk of Austria as if she were a long-lost friend and not a recent and the most Nazified of all enemies," as Herbert Matthews reported from London. And they read Bevin's speech before the Labor Party Conference and saw that his comprehension reached to France. "I can understand the French," said Bevin. "When a country has been invaded three times by Germany you have to put yourselves in their place and understand the feeling of insecurity and it is very hard not to meet what they suggest." Then Ivan sullenly noted that in the same conference Bevin regretted that he "can't understand the Russians, can't understand them at all."

Who is going to put Russia together again? Who is losing sleep over her "abbreviated means of production?" Who is lightening the burdens for millions of men and women who toiled a quarter of a century to build the basis of a better life in Russia, and now must sweat for another decade to pick up the broken bricks? Did America offer Russia a serious alternative to reparations? Did Congress propose ten billions in credits to help in Russia's tasks? Did it not, on the contrary, grant billions to Britain and France only after the State Department had convinced our party leaders that it was the only way to support anti-Soviet forces in those countries—and thus to keep them from adopting continental policies of economic barter which might help Russia?

Of course we know that isn't true. Those loans had no more hostile intent than arrangements for permanent Anglo-American joint staffs and standardization of weapons, or than our joint naval demonstration in the Mediterranean, or our common policy on the Dardanelles and on Iranian oil, or the Truman-Churchill exhibition at Fulton, or our exclusive partnership on the atomic bomb. We know absolutely that "there is no Anglo-American bloc," as the *New York Times* says, "there is only a fraternal association." But something in the Moscow air prevents the Russians from seeing the fundamental difference.

Again, we brought the countries of Central and South America into *de facto* alliance with us in the Chapultepec agreement for the general interests of world peace. Obviously the same is true when we supply these neighbors with arms, make them military equipment interchangeable with ours, train their officers and bombardiers, and arrange credits and loans with tie-ins and trade treaties.

Try as we will, however, we cannot make the Russians see what every American knows, that when Moscow makes alliances with Poland, Czechoslovakia and Yugoslavia, seeks to standardize arms, and arranges cunning trade deals, such policies stink to high heaven of power politics. Our press holds that it was wicked for Russia to retake Karelia after defeating Finland, but the Muscovite, living in isolation as he does, cannot discern why that action violated the Atlantic Charter, whereas President Truman's unilateral announcement of America's sole trusteeship rights to former Japanese islands upholds the same pact.

It is still more difficult for Ivan Ivanovitch to see that it is reactionary for Russia to lead a bloc of East European states in the UN Assembly, but that it is a sure guarantee of speedy world reform for the United States to lead China, the South American states and the British dominions in a "fraternal association." He takes it for granted that Eastern Europe should observe foreign policies friendly to the U.S.S.R., for if it did not he would think he had not defeated the enemy invaders.

Ivan hopes the UN will preserve peace, but he believes that if it is to work Russia must retain veto powers in the Security Council. Otherwise, Russia could be isolated on every major issue and decisions could be taken which would completely nullify the transcendent fact that the Soviet system holds the balance of power in Eurasia. The Russians think that if conditions were reversed, America would never abandon the veto to protect her vital interests. They think that we now insist on retaining the veto solely because of the remote possibility that we might some day be outvoted on principal issues, and have real need for it.

Such is the perversity of Ivan Ivanovitch that he doubts whether for Americans to have a monopoly to exploit the oil of 400,000 square miles of Saudi Arabia, and Britain to control virtually all the oil in Russia's neighborlands in Mesopotamia, helps to achieve a fair distribution of world resources. It follows that he fails to perceive that for Russia to seek oil concessions in Eastern Austria or Northern Iran amounts to Red imperialism and threatens the foundations of civilization. He cannot even understand why when Sweden grants credits enabling Russia to buy machinery for her looted factories it brings an angry protest from the State Department, whereas if Congress gives about a billion dollars in lend-lease and credits to Chiang Kai-shek's one-party government during civil war in China, sensible people see that this is helping to promote democracy and stabilize world economy.

"The average Russian, not the bureaucrat or the Kremlin," thought it inconsistent when our State Department demanded democratic elections of the American type in countries of Eastern Europe—where for the most part democracy never existed—but issued no démarches concerning places much nearer to us, where we have real interests. Ivan read Mr. Truman's declaration of "American world leadership" and his promise to insist upon the right of "all peoples," in Asia as well as in Europe, "to choose their own form of government without interference from any foreign sources." Then this literal-minded fellow looked for a practical application, a note from the State Department, which would implement that policy in various countries, whole continents, where we share responsibilities.

He looked on while American weapons and planes were used to reconquer the millions of inhabitants of Indo-China and Indonesia, and waited

95

to hear Mr. Truman mention "plebiscites" or "free elections," in answer to direct appeals from those peoples, but he never did. Mr. Byrnes did not tell Chiang Kai-shek we wanted him to hold a "supervised election" in China nor Mr. Bevin that he must give suffrage to the 150 million people in princely India, nor the men and women in Malaya, nor in colonial Africa.

"It makes us laugh," a Russian scientist said to me in Moscow, "to hear you always referring to Anglo-American policies as the 'leadership of the West' and to Russia as the 'East.' Isn't it a fact that you and the British together call the tune for most of Asia and Africa—say about a billion orientals? That's your 'West.' Aside from a few million people in Central Asia and Siberia, Russia's responsibilities are entirely European."

Recently Mr. Bevin remarked that Franco had killed more Spanish republicans than the British had lost in lives during the war, but neither he nor Mr. Byrnes demanded supervised elections in Spain. In fact Mr. Acheson told a press conference in November that, "Anyone who thinks the United States is going to bother with the conduct of internal operations of the Franco regime is talking nonsense."

96

Hemmed in by their "group aberrations" and their "national paranoia," as Brooks Atkinson explained it, the benighted Russians foolishly conclude that we are interested in democracy only in places where their friends are influential and where we must protect the rights of their enemies.

5

MR. ACHESON could point to the Yalta and Potsdam agreements, which obligate Russia to observe certain principles in the Balkans, in terms "as we understand them." But the Russian could insist on legality, too, and keep reminding us that we also signed documents which contained clauses we would prefer to forget. He notes that at Potsdam we conceded to Russia "all claims in respect of reparations to shares of German enterprises which are located in the eastern zone of occupation in Germany, as well as to German foreign assets in Bulgaria, Finland, Hungary, Rumania and Eastern Austria," and he approves of economic operations which ensued.

"Nor can the United States or British governments logically complain now," Ivan could read in a translation of a Demaree Bess article in *The*

Saturday Evening Post concerning such operations, "for the Russians need merely point out that these governments signed the agreements."

So Ivan thinks his government is fulfilling its Potsdam obligations. He knows that Russia is accused of dropping an "iron curtain" from Stettin to the Adriatic, and that in the case of Poland the allied press was specifically promised, "full freedom to report" developments. But he may be reassured when William L. Lawrence reports to the *New York Times* that he found "neither a barrier nor a screen" in Poland. "I was free to go where I would and see whom I would—both friends and foes of the present government," he says, and "there was no censorship of anything I wrote." And it is a fact that "Micolajzcek (opposition leader) is able to receive correspondents and denounce his own government." Or perhaps Ivan reads Demaree Bess' statement that he had no difficulty entering Hungary, "found very little mystery about what is going on," and talked to everyone he wanted to meet. Knowing that neither of these correspondents is in reality a Soviet agent, he thinks the iron curtain is an exaggerated figure of speech.

Earlier I demonstrated how the armistice

terms in effect gave Russia the authority to suppress any anti-Soviet party in the occupied states. Though Potsdam promised democratic parties a free press and popular elections, subject to military supervision, in all Germany, Soviet authorities also had the legal right to decide when a party is democratic and when it is hostile to Russia. They often took the perverse view that the two are incompatible.

A professor of Christian ethics, Reinhold Niebuhr, comes back here from Germany with a fiery eye to report that "socialist, Christian socialist and conservative Christians are putting up a fantastically heroic fight against communists." "Their prime concern is to fight communists," and they need our support, he argues. Ivan may not be a communist enthusiast at home, but he tends to think that Germans whose prime purpose is to fight communists would also like to fight Russians and he wants to put a stop to that. He feels such "fantastically heroic" Germans cannot be very friendly to him, nor repentant for their crimes. He is not bothered if in the Russian zone they are roughly discouraged.

Ivan thinks that the Red Army has given Eastern Europe more political democracy than it knew before. Finland and Czechoslovakia were the only two countries in this area that practiced our kind of democracy, and it must be admitted that Russian troops withdrew from both nations and restored native control over internal political affairs. In the Balkan countries fascism has been abolished, and now there is a multi-party system and an opposition is allowed to exist. What the Russian at home may not know is that some patriotic and anti-fascist Rumanians, Hungarians and Bulgars, who have honest differences with native communists but no intention of fighting Russia, are intimidated and discriminated against till their democratic rights are effectively cancelled.

If Ivan Ivanovitch understood that, he might mutter his sympathy with the disfranchised and behind his beard condemn stupidity and terror everywhere. But in the next breath he might, so perverted is his Asiatic sophistry, remark that American critics might be more impressive champions of pure democracy in the Balkans and Poland if they had shown similar zeal for "absolutely free elections" in some Southern states where the poll tax has legalized minority rule for generations.

The average Russian assumes that when terms

of the new treaties have been fulfilled, the Red Army will withdraw from the remaining occupied countries. He feels that enough changes have occurred in these countries to prevent them being utilized to attack Russia, but he doesn't consider them Soviet states. He takes for granted that "fascists, fascist sympathizers and collaborators" have been expropriated and removed from power. He assumes that landlords and capitalists belonged in that category (not universally accurate) and that their elimination simplified the "anti-fascist tasks" of the new governments in carrying out agrarian reforms, redistributing the land, and establishing state ownership of important means of production.

But he understands from reading Leninism that those are only "petty-bourgeois reforms," a stage in the completion of bourgeois-democratic revolution. Socialism is another thing, a long way off, and communism still more remote.

6

SATISFIED that fascism is being extirpated wherever Russia is responsible, Ivan is not much worried about other shortcomings, which would be

as inappropriate to discuss in the Soviet press as
for the *Chicago Tribune* to criticize General Mac-
Arthur. But he is well-informed on our peccadilloes
—his party lecturers see to that—and he is alarmed
beyond all reason. He knows, for example, that we
have supported a Greek regime which held fraudu-
lent elections and crushed its left-wing opposition
with terror and the help of British arms. A sus-
picious fellow by nature, he imagines that to be
somehow connected with Britain's determination
to dominate the Aegean and keep Russia locked up
in the Black Sea, behind the Dardanelles, which
England launched the Crimean War to do once
before.

I have been reading six months' accumulation of
Soviet publications and it may surprise you to
learn that Ivan also knows about Manuel Roxas.
He is aware that Roxas was a member of Japan's
puppet Philippine regime, which declared war on
the United States. He understands that it was
General Douglas MacArthur who saved Roxas
from prosecution for treason and who warmly con-
gratulated him when he assumed power in that now
dependently independent nation. He is told that
during liberation of the Philippines General Mac-
Arthur's political advisor was Andres Soriano, an

avowed fascist and former head of the Spanish Falange in Manila. He knows that by the terms of Potsdam the Supreme Commander in Japan was supposed to enforce a radical agrarian reform but that by 1947 no peasant had yet received a parcel of land. Confused by such reports, Ivan concludes that General MacArthur is not a very earnest enemy of fascism.

The Russian knows that "fantastically heroic" Italians and Japanese are also allowed to fulminate against the U.S.S.R., under our protection. He is convinced that we would never make a treaty with a Japanese government with an anti-American policy, but he is not at all sure that we would not welcome a Japanese regime hostile to Russia. He knows that openly pro-fascist groups are again active in England, France and America, and in contact with Nazi agents in Spain, South America and China. He has never seen a letter or an editorial in his own press calling for war against the United States, but he has read reprints of letters, some written by American army officers, urging war against Russia; and these appear even in our great objective newspapers. Because he does not know how to evaluate opinions expressed in our uncensored press such symptoms deepen Ivan's pessimism about the possibility of "peaceful competition between the two systems," which Molotov publicly advocates.

Instead, he worries about other matters of no importance, such as our fleet staging a demonstration off Athens during the aromatic election there or paying social calls on Turkey after the Soviet Government asks for a revision of the Montreux convention. With amazement he reads little Turkey's challenge in the semi-official paper, *Tanin*: "It is indispensable for the peace and safety of humanity that the claws and teeth of the Russian bear be rendered harmless. The world is well on the way to achieving this and Turkey is ready to accept the sacrifices of this common task of humanity."

When the United States then announces that Turkey must retain exclusive control of Russia's only exit to the Mediterranean, unless America also shares in a new administration, Ivan looks in vain for American suggestions to internationalize the Panama or Suez canals. This simple fellow cannot grasp the subtle differences involved. He gets the impression that Turkey really has no intention of removing Russia's teeth and claws herself but depends upon you and me to do it.

Although he has never heard of Frank Sinatra, the Russian adult is literate and he knows that our controversies with the U.S.S.R. all occur in Europe, the Middle East or the Far East. He notes that our Congressmen, returning from Korea, Japan, and a talk with MacArthur, warn the world of "the threat of Russian encroachment on American zones of control." He knows that we are building new naval and air bases in the Atlantic, in the Pacific islands, in Alaska, in the Philippines; arranging to share other bases with the British; and trying out super-fortresses in the Aleutians and the Arctic. His papers report that America intends to maintain naval and air forces "greater than the combined fleets of the world."

Now, the Russian reasons that his government is not having trouble with us in Mexico, Canada, South America, or in any of the great seas. All the "threat of encroachment on American zones of control" seems to be taking place on Soviet frontiers. Owing to his congenital myopia, he does not perceive that the American power outside every Soviet window is intended to give him an enhanced sense of security. Hopelessly muddled, the poor dope begins to think that he is surrounded.

7

THUS it is hard for Ivan to understand what you and I so clearly see: that in this atomic era frontiers have literally lost their meaning, and bases, spheres of influence, alliances, big armies, navies and air forces are all completely obsolete. He simply can't get it through his skull that we and the British hang on to such relics of the past only for his own protection; that in our hands they are symbols of good will; that his doctrinaire fears about the dangers of "monopoly capital" getting control of a fascist regime during a depression in the United States, and leading us into foreign war as a way out of internal dilemma, are all adolescent fancies.

Russians don't seem to realize that nuclear fission itself transformed our society overnight, changed all our thinking patterns, and made us ready to submit to a world government in which we could conceivably be outvoted. Because they know as much about scientific theory as we do, they cannot understand another thing. That with their inferior technical plant they can never trans-form matter into an atomic bomb that would enable them "to guard against all possible eventualities," as Stalin says, without being dependent on the doves of peace we are breeding in Tennessee and elsewhere.

What shall we do with this type of blockhead? He knows that the atom bomb dropped on Hiroshima obliterated 60% of the city and killed 66,000 people outright and he has been told that by 1946 America had already made another bomb 100 times more powerful. Presumably it could wipe out Moscow in one operation. Why can't he see that there is no connection between that fact and his need to keep two million troops mobilized in Europe? Surely he must realize that the most his army could do, in the event of war, would be to occupy Europe and Asia and make it necessary for the atom warriors to erase all the cities and citizens outside the Western hemisphere, in order to achieve "victory"?

By now it may be assumed that we have enough Oak Ridge bouquets stored away to blow the rest of the earth to kingdom come. That thought doesn't disturb Mr. Baruch because we know our armed forces could never conceivably go to war except in self-defense. But Ivan is scared; and beneath his bravado Comrade Molotov is scared

too. I know, because I was in Russia on Hiro-
shima-Day and after, and I saw fear creep back
into men's eyes before they had really looked on
peace.

Why? The Russians are still reeling from a
catastrophe visited upon them by a nation which
signed a pact never to make war against them.
All you have to do is imagine that conditions were
reversed. Suppose Russia had bases in Mexico and
Canada, the world's largest navy and biggest long-
range bombers, and the equivalent of something
like two billion tons of TNT condensed in a few
hundred little packages ready to be dropped anywhere on command. Suppose we were communists
and they were capitalistic Russia. Would we feel
safe just because Russians believed in private
enterprise?

In view of what Ivan knows he cannot think we
are serious when we speak of fearing "an attack
by the Soviet Union." He has difficulty reading
signs of intensified militarization into such moves
as demobilization of 60% of the Red Army and
reduction of defense expenditures from 40% to
20% in the 1947 budget. Nor does he think the
400 million dollars budgeted for science is unduly
alarming. After all, he does know that his govern-

ment spent half a billion dollars in medical research which resulted in the Roskin cure for cancer of the breast. Our Congress, he notes, would not appropriate 100 million dollars to fight the same disease, which killed twice as many Americans during the war years as were lost in battle; yet it cheerfully spends billions on the atom bomb.

Ivan Ivanovitch lives under a dictatorship and has access only to a censored press and selected books. Many of the "group aberrations" I have traced above are attributable to lack of comparative information. We in America, who have an uncensored press, unrestricted community with the truth, and enjoy all the four freedoms, must make allowances for Ivan's ignorance.

There is just a chance that in some things—despite their bad manners and irritating Marxist fundamentalism—the Russians may even have a case. While that possibility exists, and while there is an opportunity to familiarize Soviet representatives in the UN with the essential facts of life, we should examine all their arguments and expose their fallacies. We should not despair of finding a basis of compromise.

Even if we exercise the patience of saints, however, how shall we convince the Russians that everything our administration does proceeds from a firm conviction of the "inevitability of peace"? Does not Soviet policy operate on the antipodal theory of the "inevitability of war"? This question has to be answered, and in the following pages I shall be rash enough to attempt it.

[3]

WHY STALIN MUST HAVE PEACE

APPARENTLY a number of war-talk experts
have but recently learned that Lenin, more
than two decades ago, warned his followers that
the prolonged existence of the Soviet system "side
by side with imperialism is unthinkable; finally,
either one or the other will be victorious." Until
that happened, he feared, conflicts with the "bourgeois states" would be "unavoidable." He also
thought that a capitalist encirclement was in formation. "All the events of world politics," he said,
"are inevitably concentrating on a struggle of the
world bourgeoisie against the Soviet Russian
Republic."

Another belated discovery among prophets of
early apocalypse is a collection of Stalin's old
writings and speeches called *Problems of Leninism*,
which was first published in 1926. In it, you may
be sure, "the faithful disciple" did not contradict
the master's brave estimate of the future.

What is often overlooked, however, is that Lenin
died in 1924, and that his dark thesis emerged
during and after the Russian civil war, under con-

ditions which offered a certain amount of supporting detail. Memory is brief and people forget that fourteen nations (including Britain and the U. S.) had intervened against the great revolution; that the allies had torn the Baltic territories from Soviet Russia, after their conquest by Prussian Junkers, to create two buffer states entirely new to the map of Europe; that they had, till not long before Lenin's death, supported with armed force a congeries of depraved White Russian generals in Siberia; and that France and Britain had helped Pilsudski to set up a dictatorship in Poland and backed Mannerheim in counter-revolutionary war in Finland. They forget that Churchill was then calling upon Christendom to help "smash the Red nest before the hen lays any eggs," and was arming, financing, and equipping, from official funds, bands of White Russians, Poles, Ukrainians and other enemies of the Bolsheviks for what he thought was a holy mission.

It seemed that a certain amount of encirclement did actually exist in the early days. Subsequent triumph of reactionary dictatorship throughout much of Europe, continued maneuvers by Anglo-French friends of fascism to effect an alliance against Moscow, eventual formation of the Axis, and the Munich Pact, were major trends which nourished Russia's national paranoia right down to the Nazi invasion. How much Moscow helped to make the thing it feared a reality, by fostering social revolution in Europe, is another matter.

In Lenin's own time, however, the Soviet Government never in practice operated on the fatalistic assumption that nothing could be done about the danger that he foresaw. Lenin himself once seriously considered rejoining the allies in the war against Germany, in exchange for recognition and a seat at the peace conference. Even in days when imminent world revolution was still an article of faith among bolsheviks, Soviet diplomacy pursued the hope that international war could be avoided, or at least be delayed, diverted or localized. Lenin organized the Comintern originally with the hope that it might become the general staff during an international revolutionary situation. But when, after numerous rebuffs, Russia was finally admitted to the League, the Comintern was slowly transformed in the interests of Litvinov's vain agitation for "collective security."

It should be remembered that it was Litvinov who, before the rise of the Third Reich, proposed universal disarmament. It was he who first defined the term "aggressor state," in language similar to that adopted at Nuremberg, and worked to create an "anti-aggressor front" to avoid a major catastrophe. In the cases of Abyssinia, China, Spain, Austria, and Czechoslovakia, Russian proposals were not defeatist but were based on the belief that timely co-operation among "satisfied" powers could prevent war.

2

THE fact is that in *realpolitik* the state, like the rational individual, does not permit theory to interfere with practical struggle for survival—and no one can doubt that Stalin has no more to gain today than he had yesterday by combined assault of the world against him, while he has everything to gain by peace.

It is true that Lenin and Stalin wrote that capitalism leads to imperialism, imperialism breeds wars, and peace is attainable only through world revolution; and that remains the official dogma of the Communist faithful. Theoretically, that is a threat; but, in so far as our Christian faith rests on the gospels, it might hold similar alarming portent for the non-Christian peoples. We all know that Matthew, for instance, represented Jesus as

116

an agitator who came not to bring peace but a
sword, and "to set a man at variance against his
own father, and the daughter against her mother,
and the daughter-in-law against her mother-in-
law," and thus to make "a man's foes be they of his
own household." The poor among us also remember
Christ's opinion of those who wear "fine raiment,"
and who it is that a camel shall pass through a
needle's eye sooner than.

Many a nation was conquered under sanctions
supposedly contained in the gospels. In our own
memory President McKinley justified suppression
of the Philippine independence movement after an
all-night session of prayer in which God revealed
to him that it was our duty to Christianize the Filipinos—a mission which had already detained the
Spanish there for nearly three centuries.

Practical considerations have now persuaded
most Christian nations to abandon Inquisitional
methods of realizing ultra-literal interpretations
of the Bible, however, and state policy no longer
officially supports use of the Church as a fifth
column abroad. Similar laws apply to any evangel.
Experience comes quickly with responsibility in our
times, and Russians of the Marxist faith are losing
some of their fundamentalism to the wisdom of

maturity, and an eclectic interpretation of the words of the master. Dissolution of the Comintern did not end communism as an international movement, but it did give official recognition to what had already long been an observable fact: that stability in the Soviet Union's relations with the great capitalist powers was to her of greater concern than the fate of the communist parties which they sheltered.

Karl Marx was a complex personality. He was an economist, a great student of history, a sociologist, a scientist familiar with the theory of his day, a dialectical materialist who held metaphysics in contempt, and a first-rate correspondent for the *New York Sun.* He was also a revolutionary zealot, but he was touched with the necessity for subjective speculation that affected innumerable prophets. Thus it happened that he founded not only a school of politico-economics which profoundly influenced the modern world, he founded a religion as well, with its own book of revelations.

Marx was among the more practical religious leaders, however, for his method provided the means of discarding or revising his own prophecies when they proved at variance with experience. He showed quite convincingly that man as an indi-

118

vidual makes his own world but that he makes it
only in accordance with his own history—his past
and his present—in a relationship that constantly
changes. Both he and Lenin undoubtedly would re-
examine many of their speculations if they lived
as politicians today. Marx would certainly recognize, for example, the enormous importance in
man's history of such matters as electro-dynamics
and nuclear physics, and draw new conclusions.

Before the establishment of the Soviet state,
Marxists assumed that revolution would come first
as a result of a universal crisis and "breakdown"
of the whole capitalist system. It would start in
the advanced industrialized countries and immediately spread on an international scale. The idea
that it could occur in a backward country, and
alone, was not seriously discussed. In corollary,
Marx never anticipated a prolonged "proletarian
dictatorship"; once social revolution had tri-
umphed there would be complete individual freedom and democracy because state power, or coer-
cion, would cease to exist; there would be no need
for it.

Lenin also assumed that world revolution must
come quickly, or the Soviet state would collapse.
The whole fascist development occurred after his

death. He did not foresee it and he was also quite
unable, therefore, to believe that during that pre-
dicted assault by the world bourgeoisie on Russia
the "proletarian state" would have the mightiest
"imperialist powers" as its dependable allies.

3

Russia has certainly not "abandoned communism" nor Marxism today, but either explicitly or
implicitly it acknowledges that many early Marxist
speculations have been proved erroneous. Stalin
long ago officially set aside the theory of the "withering away of the state," which was Marx's closest
approach to a promise of heaven. In a new edition
of his works published this year Stalin writes a
preface in which he admits that prophecies of si-
multaneous universal revolution, of socialism
coming first in western countries, as deflected in his
own writings, were "youthful indiscretions." Now
it is clear that the "breakdown of capitalism" was
much farther away than they thought in those
days. It is clear, too, that the Soviet system is
more likely to be copied first in backward economies, Stalin says, than by highly industrialized
ones.

A generation ago Marxists considered the

church and state irreconcilable; now the Orthodox Church in Russia is officially subsidized and the right to worship is guaranteed. Marx and Engels attacked bourgeois marriage and the family; today in Russia both are protected and stabilized, by laws which resemble those in "bourgeois states." Lenin condemned "Great Russian nationalism" as a product of bourgeois society; it has been somewhat revived because experience showed that it possessed values necessary to strengthen the state. Marx hated privilege and inequality of all kinds and believed in a society where each should receive "in accordance with his need." Marxists of the Stalinist school now contend that for our time equality can exist only in so far as "the work performed" is equal.

In Lenin's writings there are no laws for the correct behavior of former Comintern leaders, such as Molotov and Manuilsky, should they find themselves sitting in the councils of the capitalist powers, leading discussions and taking the chair as peers. Likewise, in Lenin's day it would have seemed inconceivable that the Red Army could occupy half a dozen countries of Europe and Asia and not establish proletarian dictatorship in them, but withdraw instead to honor agreements with the "imperialist jackals."

So much have conditions changed that Stalin could boldly reject the fear that has haunted a generation of Russians to declare in answer to Alexander Werth's question, "I do not think that the ruling circles of the U. S. and Britain could create a capitalist encirclement of the Soviet Union even if they so desired, which, however, I cannot affirm." Instead of renewed warnings of "inevitable conflict between the two systems" he asserts that "possibilities of peaceful co-operation, far from decreasing, may even grow."

Some people may prefer to believe that Stalin does not mean what he says, that he is practicing communist duplicity and actually girding his loins for predatory war. In that case, why take any of his statements seriously—gloomy or halcyon? The truth is that Stalin could no more make such pronouncements irresponsibly, contradicting former dogma and without regard to effects on state teaching, than President Truman could publicly repudiate the Holy Trinity with no thought of internal political consequences.

But it is not my advice now to place one's faith in the Kremlin's words alone, any more than it was wise to do so when they were more discouraging. We waste too much time talking about whether Stalin wants war or doesn't, as if it were up to him.

122

A first law of politics is that all power is limited by
the problems of its control and all doctrine is modified by the practice of power. Let us see how and
why Stalin is no exception to that.

Ideological dogma did not trouble the tough-
minded men in the Kremlin when the war revealed
that they had real interests in common with the
"capitalist system." Rebuking critics within his
own party who were whispering of possible "imperialist betrayals" during the conflict, Stalin justified his policy with a homely but memorable phrase.
"The logic of facts," he said, *"is stronger than
any other logic"*—stronger than any dogma as
such.

Today the logic of facts just as plainly calls for
"peaceful co-operation." Foreign policy cannot be
divorced from domestic policy and the materials
with which it must work. In the case of Russia the
facts reveal a nation incapable of fighting a major
aggressive war against the United States, whose
help she needs for her own recuperation. In terms
of victory, of political potential, Russia is the
mightiest power on two continents. But however
much *Red Star* may boast, or Molotov strike atti-
tudes, they know that Russia is indubitably weak
and convalescent from terrible wounds. Every man
in the Kremlin understands the limitations of

Russia's own power today and fully realizes that war with America could mean complete disaster.

Theoretically, a choice of means existed, for Marxist-trained leaders, in overcoming the vast problems which faced the Soviet Union in 1945. On the one hand, the situation offered tempting opportunities to integrate Russia's economy with all Europe and Asia, through armed promotion of revolutionary class war. In China there was an army of more than a million loyal communists, with an immense popular following which could have been multiplied tenfold, with Red Army direct support. In the west communism also had enough followers to enable Russia to arm a revolution aimed at proletarian seizure of power, a bolshevized Europe, and the creation of an expanded Soviet empire. Coupled with subversive and revolutionary activity in all countries, such a program could have thrown the entire world into a convulsion the outcome of which no man could foretell.

But Soviet leadership rejected that way out of its dilemma, in the main respected agreements with the capitalist powers as the focus of post-war stability, and where necessary put a firm brake on revolutionary extremists. When I was in Poland during the Lublin government period, for example, there was a strong demand—from Polish socialists as well as communists—for an anti-clerical movement, outright confiscation of church estates, and disfranchisement of the priesthood. Stern Russian opposition quashed it. The same thing happened in the case of Rumania and Czechoslovakia. Some radicals in the Balkans favored forced collectivization of the land, complete state ownership of industry, and suppression of all conservative opposition. Moscow refused to support such "proletarian dictatorship" in any country it occupied and instead —however clumsily and imperfectly, from the "bourgeois" point of view—adhered to the Yalta and other undertakings which promised "bourgeois-democratic" structures, and urged communists everywhere to "legalize" and to co-operate in coalition reform governments.

Faced with the historic chance to meet its problems by sponsoring universal revolution, in accordance with doctrinaire aims, or risking renewed capitalist encirclement, the Politburo chose to "gamble" on that co-existence of the Soviet system "side by side with imperialism," which Lenin once described as "unthinkable."

Stalin only gave expression to what was a demonstrable necessity, therefore, from the Soviet viewpoint, when he reiterated to Alexander Werth that "Communism in one country is perfectly possible" and that his policy was based on belief that the dangers of war could be eliminated. And Stalin's speech of February, 1946, held the key to the Soviet domestic policy which governs foreign policy because he outlined the true magnitude of Russia's internal tasks and the way the Kremlin hopes to meet them.

4

In an earlier chapter I pointed out that approximately seven million Russian soldiers were killed in the recent war; perhaps as many more were partly incapacitated; and millions of civilians were also lost. Six million homes were destroyed, or the equivalent of all the living space in our fourteen largest cities. Industry, transportation and agriculture were so badly crippled that full recovery of prewar capacities cannot, under the most favorable conditions, be attained before 1950.

The need for external help to overcome problems left by the war was tremendous and urgent, and such aid could have come only from two sources: loans or gifts from America, or reparations and loot from defeated states. In the absence

126

of the first, which Russia's own policies did little to encourage, the Kremlin undoubtedly over-reached itself in gathering in the birds near at hand. When it is all added up, Russia has not really got enough useful booty to compensate her for the political opportunities she sacrificed by collecting it. At the same time her industrial removals have boomeranged somewhat, because resulting economic dislocations in the occupied countries have so handicapped their economies that they can be of little real assistance in the gigantic tasks of Russian reconstruction.

The new fifteen-year plan forecast by Stalin is actually a return to schedules laid down in 1941. At that time it was hoped that by 1956 Soviet labor productivity in the heavy industries might reach the level attained in the United States in *1929*. That is, the Russians then aspired to catch up, some three decades later, with our 1929 output of iron, steel, coal, oil and electric power. The war drastically interfered. Russia would by now have passed every country except the U. S. in steel production, but instead, even with the new Urals furnaces working, capacity dropped from 21 million tons to 15 million in 1945. In the same period American capacity increased by 50 percent.

With improved technical methods, it is expected that the original 1941-56 Soviet plan can, if recovery and reconversion are completed by 1950, be more than realized ten years later, or by 1960. The "new, mighty upsurge in national economy" demanded by Stalin envisages a trebling of pre-war industrial production, fifteen years from today.

"We must achieve a situation," he said, "where our industry could produce annually up to 50 million tons of pig iron, up to 60 million tons of steel, 500 million tons of coal, and 60 million tons of oil." Contrast this with America's *present* capacity of 60 million tons of pig iron, 90 million tons of steel, 700 million tons of coal, and 230 million tons of oil.

It may be that American capacity will drop back, since we have no plan to the contrary. But laws which have influenced development so far presumably could put us far ahead of Russia in all those basic industries, and important new ones, by 1960. In other words, Soviet industrial growth as the necessary basis of war offers us no visible threat whatsoever—provided our own system continues to exploit its potentials.

Countless other obstacles today stand in the way of Soviet leadership, including urgent economic,

128

social and political tasks which make our current worries trivial by comparison. Food is still far from abundant. Instead of being eliminated, as promised, bread rationing in Russia will continue in 1947, two years after the war. Late in 1946 the ration was actually reduced and prices of food staples had to be trebled.

Lend-lease food from America supplied a big part of the Red Army during the latter half of the war. This help ceased just at a time when millions of returning war prisoners and slave-laborers presented new mouths to be fed. Harvests in the Ukraine and White Russia this year dropped back to pre-revolutionary figures. War losses of work animals, tractors and farming tools, combined with the fact that in many areas women and children are about the only labor left, will make the Ukraine, once Russia's breadbasket, a grain-importer for some time yet.

For four years practically *all* Soviet production was devoted to war ends. Great emphasis is now placed on consumer-goods production, but even minimum needs cannot be satisfied for several years. Despite all the "trophy clothes" sent back from occupied Europe, Soviet families often share a single pair of good boots, a single warm coat, or a party dress or suit. One American economist in our Moscow mission estimated that the Soviet population could absorb and put to immediate use our entire output of consumer goods for three years, before all families were "adequately" supplied with essentials.

When one penetrates beneath propaganda claims it is clear that reconversion has not gone ahead as rapidly as expected, owing among other factors to lack of imports of American machinery. Reconstruction in some basic industries in the Ukraine lagged behind schedule as much as 60% in 1946. Personnel remains a grave problem. Purges in industrial management exposed sabotage, incompetence and inefficiency overlooked during the war. Thousands of technicians and skilled workers were killed, and newly trained reserves lack necessary experience. Above all, a heavy weariness lay upon the land. Despite an acute shortage of labor the Kremlin had to take cognizance of the public mood by restoring an eight-hour working day and annual vacations with pay, and by offering increased wages and new incentives.

There are big gaps in the lines of teachers, doctors, laboratory workers, scientists, all professional people. Thousands of trained political leaders were lost or purged and the party ranks have not yet been satisfactorily reformed. In the Ukraine and White Russia turnover in party personnel has in many cases run from 90 to 100 percent. Problems like re-indoctrination of returning veterans and war prisoners, and resettlement and rehabilitation of refugees and repatriated workers, placed severe demands on Soviet officials responsible for production.

Russia has useful work to offer to every soldier in the Red Army today. There seems no reason to suppose that any more men are being kept mobilized than the minimum deemed necessary for political responsibilities assumed by the state, nor to doubt claims of a 60% demobilization in 1946. Soviet defense expenditure was reduced by half, for 1947. It may also be symptomatic that compulsory military training has been dropped in the primary schools, and time devoted to it in secondary schools greatly reduced.

One reassuring fact, too often ignored in guessing at Russia's intentions, is that the Soviet Union is peculiarly self-sufficient, both because of her abundant natural resources and the economic system with which she exploits them. She does not need foreign markets for capital investment; she can absorb all she has for many years to come. She does not need colonial markets in which to sell her goods, which likewise can be wholly consumed at home. She need not fear overproduction and underconsumption; with a planned economy, distribution can always balance output.

The Russian people, the millions of peasants who fight the nation's wars, well know there is plenteous land and wealth in the earth for all men at home. They want to stay there to plant and harvest ever-richer crops, not to seek "glory" in conquest abroad. The latter has neither traditional appeal to the Russian "soul," nor practical appeal to a Stalinist-educated peasant of today. The Russian people had no illusions about war even before the atom bomb; now, nothing could drive them into the support of major military adventure: not greed for land, nor resources, nor crusade for ideological supremacy.

I think Stalin really meant it when he stressed that very fact about the world of 1947. "Even if its government were anxious to do so," he said when asked about the danger of war, "not a single great power could now raise a large army to fight another great power, because now one cannot possibly fight without one's people—and the people

are unwilling to fight. They are tired of war."
Above all, *"There are no understandable objectives
to justify a new war!"* My exclamation point, but
Stalin's words.

Dwarfing everything else, of course, in a study
of Russia's ability to make war on America—or to
begin aggression anywhere which could lead to
such a conflict—are the appalling implications of
atomic power. First, Russia has not yet learned to
make atom bombs and it may be some months, or
even several years, before she learns the trick. But
our own scientists have undoubtedly convinced the
Kremlin that no nation can survive in a future war
without such weapons, and have them our allies
undoubtedly will. The important thing is that
Russian leaders likewise know, as our scientists
have by now also convinced all sane men among
ourselves, that even if and when they master complete knowledge of atomic warfare, they could not
hope to emerge as "victors" from a third world
conflict in a condition any less mutilated than the
vanquished.

All those conditions have created in the mind
and spirit of all the Russian people an unprecedented receptivity, and an unprecedented need,
for any proposals which offer mankind surcease

from war, and permanent peace. Far from ignoring that sentiment throughout the country, the Soviet government seeks to exploit it to the utmost and harness it behind plans for reconstruction and promises of plenty, in speedy realization of "communism in our time."

5

IN VIEW of such controlling facts, then, Soviet diplomatic strategy, and the hazards entailed by some of her methods in Europe as well as at the conference table, became all the more incomprehensible to some people. Why didn't Molotov stop bluffing, frankly admit that Russia is weak, beg us to come in and help, and quit mixing in politics beyond Soviet frontiers?

That is to take altogether too naive a view of *realpolitik*. The harsh truth is that trust between nations has always been a relative term; it is merely closer at some moments than others. Every intelligent foreign policy must always keep open alternative courses which can be pursued if the principal line fails. Today great nations may earnestly strive to create a situation where trust can prevail, but no power can place all its reliance on that hope

134

alone until a new alternative, should that hope fail, actually exists in the form of appeal to an effective international agency of law enforcement.

In earlier paragraphs I suggested some reasons why the Russians, both as nationalists and as Marxists, distrust a world of *Pax Americana*. As long as they do, and no other alternative exists, they will use what practical means are available to modify it, or to attempt to isolate America where possible or necessary—as indeed we seek to isolate Russia on issues important to us. Depending on where you sit, Russian fears may or may not seem cogent. But they do explain why the Soviet leaders (as our own) will not unilaterally sacrifice any interest vital to national defense, or cheaply give up any semi-vital interests, or lightly abandon political or propaganda techniques useful to keep a pulse alive in alternative courses of action.

What went on, then, throughout the London, Paris and New York meetings, was necessarily an extended process of political maneuver, bargaining, trading of concessions, and a whittling down of one alternative for another, to write important statements of new power relationships. And this process continued in Moscow in March, just as it will continue in the UN, until and unless national

interests and the securities identified with them
can be fully reconciled, and new frontiers can be
stabilized, and history works out definitive forms
to fill the huge political vacuum left by the collapse
of old orders of life in Europe and Asia.

Most of the time the public's view of these historic negotiations with Russia have been so obscured by propaganda and counter-propaganda
that it has mistaken myths and folklore for main
purposes or objectives, and observers often seemed
victims of similar confusion. In each country the
press played the role of complete advocate of its
own diplomats' order of the day, with never a
blush when the *dénouement* later proved the validity of another side to the case. In the Soviet papers
I read that it was always our "atomic diplomacy"
or "imperialist war-mongers" that blocked all
progress toward agreements. Over here the overwhelming published comment blamed the Russian
delegates alone for blotting the page of peace; the
Russians were determined to remain aggressive, it
seemed, until capitalism was overthrown everywhere.

That does not mean that our press as a whole
or even a large section of it is deliberately intent
on fostering enmity between the two nations, but

it does mean that some observers with access to millions of readers were poorly equipped to judge or interpret Russia for them. And there are signs that many Americans are beginning to suspect that. In November, 1946, the Denver University national poll revealed the significant fact that only two out of ten Americans believed our press was unbiased in its treatment of Russia and her policies, while only 17 out of 100 thought Russia alone was responsible for our failures to agree. I have some reason to suppose that if a similar poll could be conducted in Russia (which it could not), a high percentage of Soviet citizens would express similar skepticism concerning their own papers.

Certainly one of the reasons why it has taken so long to write the new peace is that for the first time in history it is being sweated out—largely at our insistence—before the eyes and ears of the whole world. If the public had learned the results of various conferences in the form of finished communiques at the end of behind-doors sessions, instead of reading daily accounts of endless bickering, accompanied by woe-unto-us lamentations by too many columnists supplied with Broadway horoscopes, we might have been better aware of the real progress made.

Nevertheless, it was part of a necessary education for us to look over the diplomats' shoulders—good for everybody, to be forced to listen to the other fellow's point of view. For if the etiology of our disagreements with Russia was revealed by all these conferences, so were substantial horizons of hope. Overriding all our differences in importance now is the fact that we did debate them in chambers of peace and we did negotiate with words, not with arms. A living synthesis of new contradictions of power has been worked out in terms of agreements functioning within sets of definitions that never existed before.

None of the major factors which determine Soviet foreign policy have radically changed, however. After the satisfactory conclusion of the foreign ministers' conference and UN sessions in December a theory spread here that some great burst of light had suddenly descended on Molotov and brought about an abrupt "new line" in his policy, which made the agreements possible. Such a notion is belied by many things but above all by the fact that the Soviet foreign program, like every aspect of life in that state so strange to us, is seldom improvised.

The strategy of Soviet foreign policy forms an

138

organic part of state planning and it operates within a scheme which allows for modification of tactics, but not for sudden reversals or transformations of strategy, as is often supposed. The Kremlin has maximum and minimum objectives on every issue, thought out in advance; only the element of timing, the correct moment at which to concede, is a major imponderable. The Kremlin is not open to persuasion or conversion but it *is* open to bargaining. Hard as it is on the nerves of our diplomats to learn this habit—which fits much of Europe as well as Asia—it may prove worthwhile if it leads to peace. And if we take the trouble to see things on a string of time rather than as a point in headlines, it is clear there has been reason for optimism right along.

"In the attempt to establish workable relations with the government of the Soviet Union," Brooks Atkinson warned us some months ago, "we have to abandon familiar concepts of friendship." Atkinson is a thoroughly honest critic held in wide esteem, and quite a few people were frightened by his dictum that with the Kremlin *"political compromise is not wanted, is not possible, and is not involved."* If that literally were true then the outlook would indeed be hopeless. But facts show us

that although the Soviet government does not
want compromise (do we?), in practice it has not
only found it *possible*, but has become deeply *in-*
volved in political reconciliations with the capitalist powers. I have traced some of the compromises
made before and during the war. Observe a few
others, since then.

6

First of all, it has erroneously been said that
even Roosevelt, at the end, became disillusioned in
his efforts to get along with Russia and lost faith
in his own strategy. I don't believe that. Roosevelt's
great design was never one of give all, ask nothing,
either in theory or in practice. I saw the President
after he had addressed Congress on the results of
Yalta, and a few days before his death. He explicitly said that his last meeting with Stalin was the
most satisfactory he had had, and they "had got
close to speaking the same language." Stalin and
Churchill had disputed many points; but "Stalin,"
Roosevelt said, "agreed to every single suggestion
I made."

At the time, Roosevelt's report to Congress on
Yalta was received as a triumph. He had made
concessions, but so had Stalin; together they had

reached a synthesis. The decision to reorganize the Polish government, for example, constituted a more important compromise for the Russians than was recognized here. Other questions—the political declarations on the satellite states, the basic principles laid down for Germany, the key reconciliation of Big Three unity with the United Nations organization—all involved partial Soviet retreats from earlier positions.

At San Francisco the Russian delegation yielded on a number of semi-vital issues. For one thing, after prolonged opposition they agreed to a basic principle which represented a major retreat in their demand for unanimity in decisions reached by the General Assembly and the councils. For another, they conceded the right of any assembly member or any state to bring a dispute directly to the Security Council. They accepted defeat on another proposal significant to them: their demand to seat the World Trade Federation of thirty-five countries in the UN. As a result of many minor concessions in writing the Charter, the union of nations became a fact.

We need not go over the various concessions made at Potsdam—they weren't all on our side. Soon afterward fears were voiced that Russian troops would never get out of Iran, China, and Czechoslovakia. But at the Moscow conference in 1945 the Russians did agree to withdraw their forces from China as soon as Japanese troops were disarmed, and so did we. The Russians withdrew from everywhere except Dairen and Port Arthur, where they remain by treaty rights, but American troops were not ordered out of China till more than a year later. Red Army forces also left Iran, Finland and Czechoslovakia and by 1947 were found nowhere except in ex-enemy states, whereas British and American troops were scattered around the world in quite a few countries nominally our allies.

Pessimists frequently said that Stalin would never accept economic co-operation in Germany, but limited agreements are now operating. They feared we could never agree on a common educational policy for Germany and Austria; in Vienna an allied commission has succeeded in rewriting textbooks acceptable to all. Mr. Byrnes contended that the Russian people would not be permitted to read his replies to Molotov, but the Soviet press did print at least one in full and many in no briefer summary than that in which many of our dailies present Soviet views.

It is said that the Soviet Government keeps its

142

peoples in ignorance concerning affairs in the outside world, and that large divisions of general and
useful information are not available in Russia,
there is not the slightest doubt. Nevertheless, Moscow daily newspapers did recently devote a far
larger percentage of their total space to foreign
news than our own did. As much as three-fourths
of *Pravda* and *Izvestia* were taken up with accounts
of the Foreign Ministers Conference in New York,
and of UN sessions and related items, during that
period. True, such reports were almost exclusively
concerned with Soviet delegates' statements and
rejoinders to "opposition" powers, and included
slashing attacks on American policy. But "for
every inch of criticism of the United States in
Pravda," according to Henry Wallace, who now
reads Russian, "at least a thousand inches of anti-
Soviet criticism appeared in the American press"—
if the former Vice-President was indeed correctly
quoted by A. A. Zhdanov, in whose 1946 report to
the Moscow Soviet I came across that startling
assertion.

For a long time an agreement on Trieste was
held unattainable, but after months it was beaten
out on the anvil of discussion and mutual conces-
sion. Much despair was expressed over Soviet

policy concerning Allied-German investment in
the Balkans and the problem of re-opening the
Danube. But these "insoluble" questions were also
settled on the basis of give and take. It was said
that the Russians would never negotiate treaties
for the Balkan states; the Red Army was determined to stay on and bolshevize them. It took 122
sessions between the foreign ministers, but the
treaties were finally drafted and approved, with
official statements of mutual satisfaction. Many
solemn predictions were made that the Red Army
would never withdraw from Austria and would
find ways to betray fulfillment of the pledge of
freedom to that state. But Soviet forces there have
been steadily reduced, and exactions for their support cut by 90%. The Russians agreed to negotiate an Austrian treaty and expedite joint allied
withdrawal. Once that occurred, Red Army forces
would disappear from the Balkans.

We were told by some pundits that Stalin was
determined to out-arm the world; let no one whisper
the word disarmament; that would be appeasement.
Yet the fact remains that it was Russia that offered
the first disarmament proposal to the UN and
called for a general census of armies, preparatory
to formation of a world police force. Then it was

pointed out by informed opinion that it would be impossible to reach a disarmament agreement with the Russians because they would never reveal the output of their own arsenals nor accept a UN inspection system. Still, they did go along with those propositions, and somewhat ahead of us.

The implication of Molotov's troop census proposal was that any nation stationing troops in foreign countries should be held strictly accountable to the UN. That would not seem to be a suitable aim for a Red Army which is said to be only waiting for Anglo-American forces to pull out anywhere in order that it may rush in. Similar happy augury might be read into Russia's strong stand in the UN against South Africa's attempt to annex new territory, and the efforts of other states to annex former mandates. Judgments of this kind work both ways, as Moscow is well aware.

7

I would be the last person to contend that Soviet compromises have been easily achieved, or can be in the future, or to deny tribute to the important function of American political opposition to Soviet policies and methods, or to ignore concessions which Moscow exacted from us, in turn. But we need not lament any of that. Only the politically ingenuous will imagine that voluntary agreements binding governments to common action are ever achieved except on the basis of reciprocal concessions.

What is obvious, if the foregoing summary is correct, is that far-reaching agreements have been made with Soviet Russia that worked in the past and hence can be made to work in the future, by the use of mutual compromise. And the reason is obvious, also, to anyone who examines history without bias: Soviet diplomacy ultimately is governed by the logic of acts and not by theoretical abstractions. By the same logic—provided we know quite concretely what we want, and provided it is a fair bargain between equals—we can eventually find a basis for agreement on treaties with Germany and Japan. Through mutual concessions we can also in time agree on means of international control of atomic energy.

In retrospect it is manifest that we have not gone backward but are slowly and jerkily inching forward. This period was bound to be full of shock and disillusionment to many Americans at the moment far removed in spirit from the deep inner torments seizing most of mankind. For what we have been witnessing from afar is the carpentry of a new world, "where a revolution is being completed," as Jan Masaryk said the other day, "which began a hundred years ago in France." It is going to last a long time yet and for the American people it is bound to be tough on the nerves.

But it need not lead to a chain reaction and a general earthquake; while time remains, needed social changes *can* be reconciled in a no-war world. ". . . It isn't five minutes to twelve," as Martin Sommers said in the thoughtful introduction to this discussion, "it's only about half past one— but now is the time to wage peace."

(4)

INVESTMENT

IN

PEACE

OVER a century ago an uncannily discerning French student and historian, Alexis de Tocqueville, made a prophecy in his classic *Democracy in America* which most respectable European contemporaries at the time considered sheer fantasy:

"Two great peoples," he said, "starting at different points, go forward toward the same ends: these are the Russians and the Americans. The others seem to have attained the limits that nature traced for them; these two alone go forward in a race of which the eye cannot see the limits.

"To attain his end, the American relies on the strength and reason of individuals. Russia concentrates in one man all the power of society. The one has for his principal means of action, liberty; the other, servitude. Their points of departure are different; their paths are diverse. But each of them seems called by a secret design of providence to hold one day in his hands the destinies of half the world."

Elsewhere, de Tocqueville seemed to define "the same ends" toward which the two great peoples were sprinting, when he said, "The nations of our time cannot prevent the conditions of men from becoming equal, but it depends upon themselves whether the principle of equality is to lead to servitude or freedom, to prosperity or wretchedness."

History has taken dramatic leaps in both Russia and the United States since then, moving us into new realms of power, especially with the impulses that culminated in the social revolution in Russia in 1917, and the technological revolution which began in this country in 1945. Both those events have modified the terms of de Tocqueville's prophecy; but, after making due allowances, his vision of a world divided between America and Russia still stands as an impressive revelation.

Now, it is a fact that every man sees his own fate mirrored in the policies which express the will of the two giants among the nations. Because unfolding of their vast super-power coincides with the discovery of limitless new energies which can be unlocked either for mass destruction or mass liberation, every thinking individual everywhere must find his destination predetermined by the paths these nations henceforth choose to travel. The safety of all mankind hinges directly upon relations between the United States and Russia.

So what we still call our "foreign" policy becomes in reality a "world" policy, or the wisdom and folly by which all men can dwell in peace and plenty, or may perish in flames.

I say "our" foreign policy rather than Russia's, because history has placed on us the mantle of its heaviest responsibilities since man began to organize. For if it is true that there are really only two "great" powers in the world today, it is also true that America is the mightier. By every measurement of physical development, and above all by possession of the knowledge and plant to produce atomic weapons, we are momentarily in a position which every Alexander has sought and which no nation in history has ever held before. The United States has been entrusted with the necessary means —lacking only the will—to impose its authority over the entire earth.

Few of us realize that this is not just rhetoric but simple fact, and fewer still grasp all its meanings for ourselves and for other peoples. So swiftly has America left behind it a past in which honest faith in the traditions of peaceful isolation was possible, to emerge into a present in which no nation can contemplate living in isolation without fear and jeopardy, that we cannot begin to see all

153

the implications of the politico-technological revolution now fully upon us. And because public
opinion is not ready for it, we have not—however
much *Pravda* may rant to the contrary—yet
evolved an "atomic diplomacy."

Nevertheless, that is precisely what we do need,
and what we must yet attempt: a policy which
adequately reflects the conditions of a fissionable
world. In our foreign relations we must take fullest cognizance of both our power and responsibility, and frankly attempt to raze and replace
the archaic structures in which we have worked
till now.

Lest I incur the wrath of Mr. Zaslavsky, and
other party sentinels in Moscow or nearer at hand,
let me hasten to say that I do not advocate an
atomic douche for Russia, nor the threat thereof
to win our purposes. Instead, what is prescribed
here is a policy which accepts the lessons of atomic
science; that this is an organic world we live in, a
world of cause and effect, action and reaction,
where all things are interdependent parts of a
general scheme of nature and man, where mutation
must and does go on constantly. Change can occur
either spontaneously, in a break-out expending
itself in destructive violence, or if the forces in-

volved are understood and properly guided by men of good will it can result in benefits for human society.

By "atomic diplomacy" I don't mean *Pax Americana*, or American Century, or neo-imperialism. I mean, in contrast to a hit-or-miss, muddling-through policy of improvisation, lacking any long-view perspectives, rather a planned policy based upon the known political, economic and social needs of the American people, and providing for ways and means of peacefully reconciling those needs to the varied impulses and real needs of other nations—in the immediate situation, especially Russia. A policy which starts with the premise that all our stupendous costs of war could have been devoted to constructive ends *if* we had spent enough time and money and energy in supporting international co-operation to keep the peace. I mean a policy which recognizes, as the significance of isolationism abandoned, the explicit lesson that external peace and the prosperity of other nations are inseparably linked with our own domestic peace and internal prosperity. A policy, therefore, which accepts international obligations on as high a level of importance as domestic obligations.

2

In the past it could be said that a well-intentioned nation might properly ascribe two legitimate functions to its foreign policy: first, to help create the best possible conditions for its own national security; second, to maintain and enlarge trade relations with friendly countries. But in this era it is no longer enough—it is indeed dangerous— to define promotion of national security and trade as the sole objectives of foreign policy. By themselves both are now anachronistic. Today it is necessary to link them at every point, to integrate them, and it is necessary to co-ordinate them, still further, with a new function which must take precedence over everything else.

That third function or aim of foreign policy— now imperatively the first—must be to create such an environment that the need and desire for armed supremacy of one nation over another nation shall become as obsolete as such motives are in relations between these United States. "The major concern of each of us (U.S.A. and U.S.S.R.) should be the promotion of *collective* security, *not* the advancement of individual security."

156

The italics are mine, but the words are President Truman's, from his January address to Congress. Speaking them, Truman reaffirmed our United Nations pledge to "unite our strength" with other nations "and to maintain international peace and security." Both avowals set a new precedent in foreign policy. Both imply recognition of responsibility to mankind for our political actions, both of commission and omission, rather than to one nation alone.

Instead of passive measures which fitted a role of isolationism in the past, we now need an active policy to promote a co-operative world. Instead of a foreign policy of wait-and-see-what-the-other-fellow-does, which is a policy of "reaction" in the pure sense of the word (an immovable obstacle never acts but only "reacts," when external force is applied to it), instead of that, we need a policy of initiative. Instead of preoccupation with the effects of men's struggle for liberty and equality everywhere, we need a policy addressed to causes, and we need concrete remedies for each. Instead of a static philosophy of the sanctity of the status quo, a doctrine of the "completed universe," which is nowhere supported by the facts of natural life, we need a philosophy of world-change and the practice of plans to help achieve it, in just, legal and democratic ways.

Now, I have never worked in the State Department but I know a number of intelligent men who have, and I can assure you, gentle reader (if you need any such assurance), that not one of them would contend that we have had such a policy in the past, nor that we have reconciled any such set of dynamic aims in our policy today. Up to the time General Marshall took over the State Department it was clear that the many facets of foreign relations had never been drawn together in any single organic plan, and that there was little real co-ordination between political, economic and national security measures, to promote the one "major concern," as President Truman describes it, of "collective security."

Let us review a few instances.

One basic reason for the failure of our diplomacy to keep us out of the last war was the entirely unscientific assumption which is still held sacred in the State Department: the myth that American economic policy in foreign countries, our foreign trade and credit policy, can have a real existence apart from political aims. In fact, it may safely be asserted that the "practical" position has been that our trade with a country carries no political responsibilities, and therefore requires no reconciliation with specific peace aims enunciated by the state.

Because of that absurd fallacy we continued for many years, after Japan began her undeclared war against China, to sell her all the war materials she could buy, and to arrange credit and exchange facilities. That would have been "logical" only if we had approved of Japan's political behavior, but the truth is that we were offering very sharp criticisms of her aggressive policy all the time our merchants were helping her to arm. The same contradiction existed in our political and economic policies toward Germany and Italy, and today it is true of Franco Spain.

At times our economic collaboration with fascists and militarists was quite indispensable for them to keep in power against internal opposition groups whose views coincided with our professed political aspirations. Yet the State Department held that our "private trade," which helped to manufacture the bombs dropped on Pearl Harbor, was not to be confused with state policy, which presumably aimed to safeguard us against such bombs.

The practice of not letting the political hand know what the economic hand doeth went right on throughout the war, and resulting contradictions may be seen on all sides today. America's unstinting economic help to Russia obviously carried with it political consequences of momentous importance. It not only greatly strengthened the bolshevik regime at a perilous moment, but it helped to project bolshevik influence farther into Europe than ever before. Hence, the Anglo-American decision to save Russia, even though it meant saving it as the center of world communism, called for immediate and precise political understandings affecting the future of Europe and Asia.

The absence of such understandings led to the dilemmas which eventually confronted the capitalist democracies wherever Soviet military power penetrated. Poland is perhaps the clearest example. Long before the Red Army entered Poland it became manifest that it would use American lend-lease weapons to arm Polish forces and set up a new regime. Yet nothing was said or done by American representatives to anticipate that fact nor to implement the political force which our economic help was creating—nothing was done till much too late.

Throughout the colonial world it was American
economic intervention, in the form of lend-lease
aid to British, French and Dutch imperial forces,
which enabled the former European imperialists
to recover power. Where the status quo ante was
not restored it was in no case because of American
political intervention, but solely because of armed
native resistance. We not only never helped the
natives in support of Truman's declaration favor-
ing independence and the four freedoms in the
colonies; as a nation we never even faced the fact
that our economic aid to the returning proprietors
in itself decided our political role in reality, as
distinguished from our political role in words.

In China after the war we have gone on working
with the old paradoxes: official American claims
of "neutrality" in internal Chinese affairs, con-
tradicted by overwhelming evidence that we have
given decisive aid to one side and one party in a
civil war that has lasted a generation. American
armed forces—land, sea and air—made it possible
for Generalissimo Chiang Kai-shek to seize strategic cities and communications in Eastern China,
which lay within grasp of the Chinese Communist
troops at the end of the war. American supplies—
somewhat more than two billion dollars' worth—

went to the Kuomintang and helped to support its troops against the Communists in North China and Manchuria. Yet at the same time our nominal political policy, as enunciated by President Truman in December, 1945, called for non-intervention in Chinese affairs and encouragement of party co-operation in a representative government.

Fundamentally it was this contradictory nature of our position which made General Marshall's failure inevitable. He could not, while representing a nation which was giving military and economic help only to Chiang Kai-shek's party in the dispute, convince the Communists that his role was solely that of a disinterested, non-partisan mediator in whose hands they could safely entrust their fate.

3

LACK of co-ordination between the economic and political functions of our foreign policy often hinges on another piece of folklore still accepted in administrative and bureaucratic circles, as well as among business men. This is the myth that international trade, conducted by private enterprise on a basis of unplanned, undirected, unco-ordinated, irresponsible, profit-motive laissez-faire, is somehow beneficial to the American people—without regard to political implications, or to the invisible costs of such trade. Investigation shows that to be a fallacy. Exports of American capital and goods are actually useful to the American people only if such commerce: 1) helps to promote co-operation for peace, or at least does not help to provoke wars; 2) thus helps to reduce the price of national defense; 3) enables us to import materials and manufactured goods or services needed for our own production or consumption requirements.

It is demonstrable that only in the above terms can the cost of defending our foreign trade be justified in the future. It is demonstrable that past policies intended to protect American access to foreign markets have often entailed outlays far in excess of any real profits to the American producers. It is obvious that there is no visible hope whatsoever of balancing off those past costs against financial returns in the future.

Take our ex-colony, the Philippines. During four decades of American occupation, U.S. exports to the islands never exceeded 200 million dollars in any year. Balance that against the fact that even before Pearl Harbor we, the taxpayers, contributed some two billion dollars to maintain our

administration and defenses there. Add to that
about a billion dollars more which we are giving
the new Philippine Government in various kinds
of compensation and war damages. Apportion a
fair share of the billions we spent in reconquering
the islands from the Japanese. Figure out, then,
how much we paid and are still paying to maintain
a picayune trade and to keep other people from
exploiting Philippine resources.

Or take China. The pre-war cost of maintaining
an Asiatic fleet alone always far exceeded any
"favorable balance" of payments in our China
trade. Our whole commerce with China for the past
100 years did not yield a net profit which distantly
approaches the sums we have poured into that
country since 1941. There was not the slightest
proof that China purely as a market would ever
pay its share, or anywhere near its share, of the
invisible costs of its "protection," if we continued
along past lines.

The entire outlay for two world wars must in a
major sense be charged against the failure of
foreign policy to prevent those wars. That whole
burden should certainly be balanced against any
conception of the "benefits of foreign trade," as
something which exists apart from its political

complexities. So should our lend-lease contributions
to allied countries, which were state-subsidized
foreign trade under the compulsion of war, and
cost us an "unfavorable balance" of something like
40 billion dollars. In the case of Russia alone we
got rid of more than 11 billion dollars worth of
goods.

Compute, if you can, how many decades of
"peaceful commerce" it would take to counter-
balance lend-lease, if regarded purely as a business
transaction!

4

THE reason we did not complain about the lend-
lease levy during the war, however, the reason
Congressmen dared not scream against it, was
because our people clearly saw that such give-away
exports were necessary to our own security. If
peace is more desirable than war, should we not
be willing to pay for it, in support of constructive
activity, at least as readily as we pay for the
destructive programs of war? It is my contention
that we should. Today our peacetime foreign trade
must have for its highest objective not private
profits, but the promotion of our "major concern"
of "collective security." In so far as economic and

trade policy cuts down the costs of maintaining armed services, and eliminates dangers of a Third World War, it has profound meaning for us.

To see the soundness of this argument as it projects into the future, consider for a moment what the National Association of Manufacturers has to say in its *NAM News* about our current state budget: "The increasing impact of foreign affairs on every phase of American business is being demonstrated by President Truman's budget estimate," the organ recently reported, "of which 85% can be attributed directly to the nation's past and present foreign policy." Mostly, of course, for maintenance of armed forces today, and to carry the debts accumulated in past wars. "If war with Russia should come," member industrialists are warned, the cost "would increase the national debt by 500 to 1,000 billion dollars."

And just as Hitler's war against bolshevism, launched as a holy crusade to save capitalism, ended by destroying that system in Europe, so in the case of an American war against the U.S.S.R., "national service will have to be imposed here immediately," according to the gloomy prophets of the National Association of Manufacturers. "This in turn would necessitate the conscription of all the productive and transportation resources of the nation and the elimination of the profit system," the *NAM News* continues, because "it would be politically and psychologically impossible to force labor to work in plants that are operated on a profit basis."

Now, let's assume that the N.A.M. is right in its fears. War with Russia would not only entail the wastage of another 1,000 billion dollars worth of labor and materials, but would end the "profit system" in the U.S. and thus write finis to capitalist democracy throughout the world. Does not such a danger make it entirely worthwhile for us to adopt, while there is still time, an economic foreign policy based on state-subsidized exports of goods and capital—a peacetime continuation of lend-lease? Provided, of course, that in exchange we can bring about universal disarmament, create an effective international police force, and bring about world co-operation for constructive ends?

Admittedly, it would mean a reversal of our conventional thinking about trade relations with other countries. Instead of regarding national security expenditures as necessary to support foreign trade we would look upon exports of capital and goods as necessary to stabilize world peace. Through an economic foreign policy which makes it possible to forestall another world war we could realize conditions in which international co-operation would not only be the correct behavior between some nations, but an inevitable way of life for all nations.

Could the U.S. by its own efforts lead the rest of the UN toward this "one-world" approach to foreign relations? How could it begin, in practice, particularly with reference to the U.S.S.R.? Here I do not propose to offer a formula, beyond briefly recapitulating what has already been said in this chapter.

We have seen that the century-old prophecy of de Tocqueville has come true; America and Russia now hold in their hands the destiny of man. As between these two powers, the U.S. at the moment carries the greater burden of responsibility because this country has an immensely more terrifying capacity to make war. By the same token it possesses a voice for peace which, if it were raised with the full resonant power and unity of the nation behind it, could nowhere be denied.

Since the fate of all nations now hangs upon American foreign policy, it has become in reality a "world" policy which other peoples have to take and cannot leave alone, whether they like it or not. It is no longer possible, therefore, to think of our relations with foreign countries merely in terms of national security and profitable trade. In the American people's sense, no benefits can be derived from any trade which does not positively help to avoid wars, whose costs otherwise nullify all "profits" made from private foreign commerce. And as Congress recognized when it ratified the United Nations Charter, and as the Chief Executive has reiterated, the interests of collective security must now be regarded as paramount to the individual interests of national security.

Two world wars have taught us that the objective of international peace cannot be found in blind adherence to the status quo. Rather, peace is a goal attainable only through movement forward in a vehicle designed to accommodate legitimate needs for change. There must be full co-ordination and organic integration in all aspects—economic, cultural, social, political, strategic—of foreign policy, based on full awareness of the interdependence of each. Trade relations with other countries, in particular, and the implementation of credit as part of economic policy, must be looked upon as specific means, in the battle for peace—a battle

waged for well-defined ends to which we have now
dedicated ourselves.

5

WHATEVER differences there may have been
between us and the Soviet Union," President Truman recently observed, "should not be allowed to
obscure the fact that the basic interests of both
nations lie in a return . . . to the essential tasks
of production and reconstruction."

No one would quarrel with that statement of
fact, but neither could anyone seriously assert that
it has been implemented in our post-war policy,
particularly in our policy of atomic armament,
aimed primarily at Russia. I think I have shown
that the Russian people desperately need peace,
and that Soviet leaders fully realize that the
country could be led to war only if there were no
other way out. But we also know that Russian
history, Marxist ideology, the catastrophe of two
wars, and deep distrust of the motives and potentials of the capitalist world, have combined to build
up a profound dread of encirclement in the Soviet
Union.

That historical background has nurtured certain
Soviet behavior in Europe which Undersecretary

of State Dean Acheson has described as "aggressive and expanding." But I think it is almost self-evident that the main aims of Soviet foreign policy are to achieve an immunity against new invasions which could again interrupt, this time perhaps forever, the "building of socialism in one country."

If we wish to eliminate the "aggressive and expanding" characteristics of Soviet foreign policy, it is in our interest to try to dispel the fears which to so large an extent motivate it. And before we say that cannot be done we owe it to mankind, and to the position of supreme responsibility which history has imposed on us, to make the attempt. Shall we be specific? Here are some proposals which, among other things, could be done at once to ease tension and anxiety throughout the world, and which seem to me entirely reasonable.

1) *Open direct Soviet-American negotiations for basic political, economic and military agreements.* Since world co-operation now depends almost entirely on our mutual comprehension, discussions at which other powers are present often merely obscure the heart of issues and dissension. There is nothing wrong with two-power talks as

long as their results are made public for the benefit of all powers.

The Soviet Government is so organized that the Politburo and the Central Committee of the Communist Party determine policy on all major questions. To reach comprehensive working agreements with the U.S.S.R. it is necessary to deal with those committees and with their titular chief, Josef Stalin. If it is true, as I have supposed, that the main historic responsibility for making and keeping the peace now lies with America, we should not be ashamed to take the initiative in calling a Big-Two Conference, or a number of conferences, where the Soviet and American heads of state, with full staffs present, can plan the peace for a generation to come. Such meetings should seek to establish the peace both in general agreements and in terms of joint programs for concrete measures whereby the UN Charter, and other mutual commitments, may be implemented in active ways.

2) *Economic collaboration with the U.S.S.R.* Preliminary conditional guarantees of American good-will should precede such a conference. Foremost among them is the need for a definite assurance of America's desire for co-operation, economically, with the U.S.S.R. on a new liberal basis laid down for all peaceful nations. The reasons

why that is in our own interest are obvious but may here be briefly reviewed.

The U.S. now possesses more than half the world's gold, industrial capacity and shipping, and nearly all the export capital available for investment. It is the only country which can extend to Russia the large-scale aid it needs, if her travail is to be lightened. But it also happens to be true that Russia could provide, for U.S. capital and industry, an export market of such magnitude— up to five billion dollars annually—that it would be of real significance in helping to maintain a balance between production and consumption in our own unplanned economy.

Economists generally agree (or at any rate the ones that impress me agree) that a crisis is inevitable in American economy within a few years— the familiar crisis of overproduction and under-consumption. Even Walter Lippmann thinks that we cannot get through more than ten years, at the outside, without being confronted with old man "trouble," as he calls it. Yet he admits the great test may come much earlier, perhaps in a matter of three years. At that time this country will find itself with big "surpluses"—especially in the case of heavy industries making durable goods and prime movers—and in desperate need of new markets in which to invest accumulated capital for which domestic markets have dried up.

Conventional "ways out" in such a situation are: a) extension of cheap state credits to foreign countries, to stimulate exports of goods, and of capital for reinvestment abroad; b) militarization of industry in a huge program of rearmament (the solution Hitler and Mussolini deliberately chose, and the solution this country involuntarily chose after 1939—and the origin of course of our present "stability" and "prosperity"); and c) state-subsidized peaceful public works programs to maintain maximum employment of labor, and to compel "communal investment" through capital-levy taxation (such as the New Deal attempted). Of these possible remedies, preventives, palliatives or appeasements (choose your own word) the first, the extension of cheap credits to foreign countries, linked with exports of American goods, offers the solution which, superficially, is least likely to disturb internal economic relationships. Combined with a program of moderate public expenditure at home, it might defer a general crisis in our capitalist economy for some time.

Hence it would be in the interests of world peace, and of stability within both countries, for us to give substantial financial assistance to Russia. Prior to the summoning of the Big-Two conference, the U.S. should announce its readiness to extend, either directly or through UN agencies, the fullest economic co-operation to the peaceful purposes of the U.S.S.R. To be exact, we should publicly declare the availability of long-term low-interest credits or loans, as well as access to American goods and technical knowledge, for use in the internal reconstruction and peaceful industrialization of the U.S.S.R.

3) *Collective Security—the price of economic collaboration.* Help in the above terms would naturally entail, and perhaps be contingent upon, a general agreement on world-trade policy. Even more important, and an essential precondition of economic co-operation, would be fundamental agreements between the two powers which would satisfactorily reconcile the thorny questions of national security and international security, viz: a) Soviet Russia and the United States must work out a satisfactory system of control, development and use of atomic energy; b) the two powers must find a formula for mutual disarmament, and jointly present it for adoption and enforcement by the UN; c) they must then lay down a schedule by

which they shall systematically "unite their strength to maintain international peace and security," perhaps pooling the armaments of which they mutually divest themselves, and placing these at the disposal of the UN Security Council, as the nucleus of an international police force to which other member nations would likewise contribute; and d) they must work out the organization of an International Inspectorate, which will have the authority to examine disarmament procedure in each country, and to secure fulfillment of terms guaranteeing the paramountcy of collective security above individual security.

4) *A common political program.* Obviously the U.S.S.R. would not agree to promote capitalist ideology throughout the world; obviously the U.S. would not be able to support Marxist ideology. But that does not entirely rule out limited political co-operation, since history has already demonstrated, in Molotov's words, that "states with widely different political structures have extremely important interests in common." And it is perfectly possible to define such interests, and to work together to uphold them on a world scale. There *is* an area of common faith, however restricted, wherein Soviet-American interests and

176

ideologies coincide. We cannot agree on the exact meaning of "fascism," it's true, but we *can* agree on manifestations of it which in practice both countries oppose. We cannot agree on an exact definition of "democracy" or "equality," but there are aspects of both which we can uphold together.

To illustrate, America and Russia could jointly oppose, everywhere throughout the world:

a) ideologies which openly preach war and aggression, and governments which sanction them;

b) ideologies which preach racial discrimination, religious persecution, suppression of equality of rights among all nationalities, and governments which sanction such behavior in law or in practice;

c) ideologies which deny freedom of educational opportunity to all, and governments which oppose it;

d) ideologies which deny working people the right to organize and bargain collectively, and regimes which prohibit it.

Other principles could be found in common. Similarly, codes of an affirmative character could be worked out for action in support of democratic states or movements which actively promote equality of opportunity, equality before the law, racial harmony, religious tolerance, non-interference of the church with the state, and doctrines of peaceful co-operation between nations on the basis of arbitration of disputes rather than resort to arms. And so on. Perhaps we should find sharp limits to practical ways of co-operating politically, but perhaps also, once fears and mutual suspicions were minimized by a program of collective security and economic collaboration, vast new fields of mutual interest might be opened up. And in those fields a true new internationalism might flower between us.

5) *Cultural exchange.* Till now the historic "apartness" of the Slav consciousness has been strengthened by Soviet beliefs that class antagonisms hopelessly divide Russia from the democracies of Western capitalism. Suspicion and distrust are manifest on both sides, but particularly in Soviet official policies which virtually prohibit free intercourse between private citizens of the two nations. If we assume that a background of basic co-operation were achieved, along lines I have outlined above, then a healthy normal intercourse could be expected to follow. A free exchange of products and personalities of Soviet and American art, music, literature and folkways, a sharing of experience and knowledge, of theory and practice

in education and educational method, in social sciences, and in natural sciences—such an exchange could greatly enrich the cultures of both nations.

Only bigoted chauvinists, or Neanderthal reactionaries, need fear such a mixture and rivalry of ideas and materials of the two civilizations, once the factor of mutual insecurity were removed from the picture. Everyone could benefit. True democrats could not but welcome a chance to share and compete with Soviet cultural attainments in an atmosphere of free inquiry and scientific search for the truth.

6

IT IS of course not my idea that such an entente with Soviet Russia could be the successful foundation of a "world" policy of the U.S. if it in any way limited or discriminated against co-operation, on the basis of the same principles, with other powers. Quite the contrary. A schedule of the kind described would most likely impress Russia only if the United States simultaneously sought the adherence of France, Britain and other democratic powers to collective security arrangements and generous economic collaboration plans. In the case of the Western powers no doubt agreement on specific measures in support of democracy, and against resurrection of fascism, as the basis of world political co-operation, could reach much farther than a Soviet-American program.

The foregoing suggestions are not intended to prescribe an infallible remedy for what's wrong with our foreign policy. Obviously they are little more than the crude outline of a new approach to Russia and to other nations. It is a demonstration by concrete means that those cynics are wrong who say that nothing can be done to improve relations with Russia because everything has been tried. That isn't true at all, and such measures as I have proposed are only one way of showing that.

Of course, even these efforts, made with the very best intentions, might fail, though it is hard to believe they would fail totally. At any rate, we would not know for several years, as such a schedule would have to develop its implementation through a process of trial and error, breaking new trails. But if in the end sincere and exhaustive negotiations achieved no results, at least we would have brought to our own people the political unity which can only grow out of moral conviction of fairness in the right and honesty of intent. It would certainly greatly improve our chances of maintaining leadership in organizing the moral and political, as well as the material, forces of the rest of mankind in a parliament of non-Soviet man.

Other criticisms can be made of what I have roughly sketched. Some people may call it "unrealistic," "too soft toward Russia," or "appeasement," which are more or less synonymous, it seems. But that would be a foolish kind of criticism of the program I suggest. For appeasement means (in the notorious sense of Chamberlainism) to satisfy the demands of an aggressor in exchange for nothing but an illusion—to increase his appetite by sacrificing your own power of resistance for only a momentary relief from anxiety. What I propose is not appeasement but bargaining on a wholesale scale, nothing paid for nothing given, but an offer of major economic help in exchange for irrevocable steps toward world peace.

True, such a policy, if (as it should be) extended toward all our allies as well as toward Russia, might cost us 40 or 50 or 100 billion dollars during the next ten to twenty years, in loans and credits which would pay interest but in the beginning perhaps bring little repayment of principal. And those sums would represent direct taxation on you and me and upon our labor power, and upon production. But when in return we secured stage-by-stage disarmament of individual nations and the arming of collective police power, it would be cheap, for my money, at twice the price.

No one could guarantee in advance that it would work. All we know is that the only alternative is quite certain to fail. I mean the illusion which many still wistfully pursue, that we can save ourselves by maintaining (at equal or greater expense) naval and air fleets bigger than the combined forces of the world, and by making bigger and better atom bombs than all others. For that "visionary" and irrational course surely by now has been shown by history to be futile, for never yet has national security been achieved apart from international security. The attempt to make one nation supreme or impregnable inevitably will lead today, as it has invariably led in the past, to an armaments race, and to that suicidal conflict which the N.A.M. predicts may cost us 1,000 billion dollars—if anyone is still left alive to pay it.

Other critics may call my proposal of "organic bargaining" merely a different name for power politics. Admittedly, that charge would have validity, for it is urged that we combine the weight of our existing strategic advantages with economic power, to attain specific political aims. But to me it has long seemed clear that there is in reality only one kind of politics, which is power politics. Ideas, ideals, public opinion, Gandhi's non-violent civil disobedience campaigns, or passive resistance, all represent efforts to mobilize moral force or public opinion, in terms of power. All play a role in politics, but they do so only when successfully linked with genuine power placed in motion for concrete aims. Similarly, economic factors everywhere also constitute political potentials and inevitably play their role. The only important question is whether moral and economic factors are consciously directed by men or whether they remain "blind force" which make men and nations their involuntary or unconscious tools.

But there is a criticism for which I confess I have no answer. It is that the policy suggested would prove utterly unacceptable to the present Congress and administration. Without being unduly cynical or pessimistic, I must acknowledge that that is all too true. For in making these remarks I have been under no illusion that General Marshall, even if he himself were fully convinced of the desirability of a dynamic American leadership (as indeed he seems to be), would now be permitted to carry it out.

Nevertheless, I have thought it worth writing down as I have, in order to show how foreign policy could—if the people would relentlessly insist upon it as an essential part of the struggle for world peace—be invoked to dispel the fear of atomic war from the earth. And if at the same time I have persuaded some readers that an intelligent foreign policy could help to satisfy the needs of internal economy, and thus modify the severity of a new catastrophe toward which the nation is now clearly being dragged, I shall feel amply rewarded.